The First Ladies

Martha Washington to Hillary Clinton

CRESCENT BOOKS

New York / Avenel, New Jersey

This 1992 edition published by Crescent Books,
distributed by Outlet Book Company, Inc., a Random House Company,
40 Engelhard Avenue, Avenel, New Jersey 07001.

Printed and bound in Hong Kong

ISBN 0-517-68785-2

8 7 6 5 4

The First Ladies

Contents

INTRODUCTION

As you read through the biographical sketches that complement the portraits collected in this book, each First Lady emerges as an individual with a fascinating background. Throughout the history of the United States, the efforts of these women have kept the country informed of the traditions and functions of the White House. *The First Ladies* contains interesting information about each of these women from their vital statistics to lively details of their personal lives and interests.

The personalities of the First Ladies were as many and varied as their attitudes and approaches to the position of First Lady. Most were wives of the elected President, but several other female relatives also served as First Lady. Each of these women brought her own inimitable style to the White House, beginning with Abigail Adams since Martha Washington never actually occupied the White House in the District of Columbia.

The full-color portraits that accompany each history are suitable for framing. This volume also contains a short history of the White House. This book is a fitting tribute to each woman who has served as First Lady and has brought her individual style and significance to the role.

Martha Dandridge Custis Washington

Served as First Lady during the term of her husband, George Washington, first President of the United States

BORN	June 21, 1731
PLACE OF BIRTH	Chestnut Grove Plantation, New Kent County, Virginia
ANCESTRY	British
MOTHER	Frances Jones Dandridge
FATHER	John Dandridge
HUSBANDS	Daniel Parke Custis (1711-1757)
	George Washington (1732-1799)
CHILDREN	Four: 2 boys, 2 girls
EDUCATION	Educated at home
AGE AT INAUGURATION	57
YEARS AS FIRST LADY	1789-1797
DIED	May 22, 1802
CAUSE OF DEATH	Natural causes

Martha Dandridge enjoyed a pleasant childhood on her parent's Virginia plantation, where she had lessons in music and riding as well as housekeeping. Graceful and confident, she moved easily in Virginia's high society. She married Colonel Daniel Parke Custis when she was seventeen, and had four children. But by the time Martha was twenty-five, two of her babies and her husband had died.

As a pretty and wealthy young widow, Martha had many admirers. She chose Colonel George Washington, and the two were married in 1759. For the next 16 years, Martha and George Washington divided their time between Six Chimneys, Martha's estate in Williamsburg, and Mount Vernon, George Washington's plantation just across the Potomac River from what is now the nation's capital. In 1773, Martha's other daughter died. When the Revolutionary War came and George Washington was made Commander of the Continental forces, Martha remained at Mt. Vernon to manage the estate.

She made many trips to her husband's military headquarters. During the hard winter at Valley Forge, she took care of the sick and wounded soldiers. She set an example for others by wearing American homespun rather than clothes made of expensive imported fabric. When her son, John Parke Custis, died of camp fever during the war for independence, his two children came to live at Mount Vernon.

When the Presidential barge first docked in New York, the new nation's capital, no one knew what to expect of the first President and his wife. But a tradition was born as "Lady Washington" waved to the crowds that lined the streets: the First Lady would be a public figure, standing before the American people at her husband's side.

Martha Washington kept her simple, amiable, and industrious ways when her husband became the first President of the United States. Although she presided gracefully over social occasions, she did not like the life of the First Lady. The temporary capitals of New York and Philadelphia never felt like home to her, and the formality of state receptions made her uncomfortable. Although she missed her quiet life in Virginia, Martha Washington fulfilled her role with dignity.

In 1797, George and Martha retired from public life and returned happily to their Mount Vernon estate. George Washington died two years later. Martha remained at Mount Vernon, living quietly until her death at age seventy in 1802. Her will freed all the slaves at Mount Vernon.

Abigail Smith Adams

Served as First Lady during the term of her husband, John Adams, second President of the United States

BORN	November 23, 1744
PLACE OF BIRTH	Weymouth, Massachusetts
ANCESTRY	English
MOTHER	Elizabeth Quincy Smith (1721-1775)
FATHER	William Smith (1706-1783)
HUSBAND	John Adams (1735-1826)
CHILDREN	Five: 3 boys, 2 girls
EDUCATION	Educated at home
AGE AT INAUGURATION	52
YEARS AS FIRST LADY	1797-1801
DIED	October 28, 1818
CAUSE OF DEATH	Natural causes

Abigail Smith's father was a Congregationalist minister who believed education was important. From childhood on, Abigail was an avid reader and letter writer. At nineteen, she married her cousin John Adams, who was a lawyer. The two shared a love for books and conversation, and John considered her his intellectual equal. They lived on his farm in Braintree (Quincy), Massachusetts, where they had five children, one of whom died in infancy.

John's law career required him to travel often. Then came the American Revolution, followed by his appointments to the Continental Congress and as an envoy to Europe. Separation became a sorry fact of life for John and Abigail. While John was away, Abigail ran the farm, managed the household, and saw to the children's education. She missed her husband terribly and wrote him often, keeping him informed of personal business and political developments at home. She advised Adams in a famous letter to "remember the ladies" while the Congress was debating the question of American Independence. Women's rights, especially in education, concerned Abigail all her life.

In 1784 Abigail finally joined her husband in Europe, living in Paris and London for nearly four years. The couple returned home and John Adams became the nation's first Vice President. Abigail worked with First Lady Martha Washington to set protocol and establish precedents for formal social functions. However, when her husband was re-elected, she returned to Massachusetts.

After her husband's election as president, Abigail brought to social occasions some of the elegant style she had experienced while in Europe. As President Adam's wife, Abigail discussed politics with him, reviewed his speeches, gave him advice, and publicly supported his policies. She had a sharp tongue and strong views, and her opinions on political issues and national leaders were thought to influence her husband. Abigail was dubbed "Mrs. President" and was often criticized for her "unladylike" ways. But her dinners and parties were lively, sparkling with witty and intelligent conversation.

In October 1800, the Adamses left the temporary capital of Philadelphia and moved to the new federal city under construction on the Potomac. The presidential home was far from complete, but with typical style and vigor, Abigail was soon ready to carry out her role as the first White House hostess.

Abigail was disappointed when John Adams was not elected to a second term. But the couple enjoyed the time they could now spend together back home in Massachusetts with their children and grandchildren. Abigail watched with satisfaction as her son John Quincy advanced in his public and political career, not knowing she would be the only woman to be the wife of one President and the mother of another. Although she was cheerful and busy, Abigail was ill for much of her last years and died in 1818, just before her seventy-fourth birthday.

Martha Washington Jefferson Randolph

Served as First Lady during the term of her father, Thomas Jefferson, third President of the United States

BORN	September 27, 1772
PLACE OF BIRTH	Monticello, Virginia
ANCESTRY	Welsh, English
MOTHER	Martha Wayles Skelton Jefferson (1748-1782)
FATHER	Thomas Jefferson (1743-1826)
HUSBAND	Thomas Mann Randolph (1768-1828)
CHILDREN	Twelve
EDUCATION	Convent School, Paris, France
AGE AT INAUGURATION	29
YEARS AS FIRST LADY	1801-1809
DIED	October 10, 1836
CAUSE OF DEATH	Stroke

By the time Thomas Jefferson became President, his wife had been dead for eighteen years. She had always been frail and became more delicate as each of her children arrived. A widow with one son when she married Thomas Jefferson, Martha Jefferson gave birth to five daughters and one son in the ten years after her marriage to the future president. Only two of her children lived to adulthood. These two daughters, Martha and Mary, were the joy of Jefferson's life after his wife died.

Martha Jefferson, called "Patsy," grew up on Monticello, the family's Virginia plantation. Not yet ten years old when her mother died, young Martha tried to be cheerful for her grieving father. Father and daughter were often together, Martha accompanying Jefferson on horseback rides through the countryside and on his business trips as well. She had the best private tutors Jefferson could find, and attended a convent school in Paris when Jefferson served as Minister to France. Martha grew up fast; her father expected a lot of her and she was anxious to please him.

After Martha married her cousin Thomas Randolph, the couple lived at Monticello, together with Martha's sister and her family. Jefferson was there less and less frequently, until finally he moved to Washington when he became President in 1801. Jefferson missed his daughters terribly. He urged them to join him in the White House, but they were reluctant to expose their young children to the unsanitary conditions of the swampy capital city.

The President was not concerned about having an official hostess. He believed in simplicity and did not hold formal receptions. Knowledgeable about food and wine, he managed his small household staff himself. Jefferson scorned protocol. Sometimes he received visitors in his bedroom slippers or muddy riding boots, and he asked his dinner guests to sit wherever they pleased. But since women couldn't attend social functions without a hostess present, Jefferson's old friend Dolley Madison often presided over state dinners. At this time, Dolley Madison's husband James was Secretary of State. Martha came to Washington with her husband and acted as lady of the house for several extended periods, earning praise for her intelligence and charm. The first child ever born in the White House was Martha's son, James Madison Randolph.

Jefferson and his daughters lived together again at Monticello after his retirement. Martha found the estate a sad place after her father's death and went to live with her daughter in Boston for a time. She died in 1836 at the age of sixty-four.

Dorothea Dandridge Payne Todd Madison

Served as First Lady during the term of her husband, James Madison, fourth President of the United States

BORN	May 20, 1768
PLACE OF BIRTH	Guilford County, North Carolina
ANCESTRY	Welsh, Irish
MOTHER	Mary Coles Payne (?-1807)
FATHER	John Payne (?-1792)
HUSBANDS	John Todd (1764?-1793)
	James Madison (1751-1836)
CHILDREN	Two boys
EDUCATION	Private tutor
AGE AT INAUGURATION	41
YEARS AS FIRST LADY	1809-1817
DIED	July 12, 1849
CAUSE OF DEATH	Natural causes

Dorothea ("Dolley") Payne's early life gave little indication that she would rise to social prominence. She was raised a strict Quaker and was taught to dress plainly, behave quietly, and avoid extravagance. After her family moved from Virginia to Philadelphia, Mr. Payne's business failed and Mrs. Payne had to make their home into a boarding house. In 1790 Dolley married John Todd, a lawyer from her Quaker congregation, but within three years both he and one of their two infant sons had died of yellow fever.

In the bustling city of Philadelphia, young Dolley attracted much attention with her gay personality and good looks. She was introduced to Congressman James Madison, and the two were married in 1794. Shunned by the Society of Friends for marrying outside the faith, Dolley was free to do things she had only dreamed of before: she wore fancy clothes, went to parties, even played cards!

While James Madison was Jefferson's Secretary of State, Dolley presided over diplomatic dinners for both her husband and the President. The special menus she prepared placed her recipes in great demand. She dressed in all the latest fashions, and women everywhere imitated her style of dress. But it was Dolley's charm and friendly disposition that made her famous, and she was soon known as the "Queen of Washington City."

When James Madison became President, Dolley continued in her role as Washington's most popular and fashionable hostess. At her lavish parties she often helped to soothe political tension, since she was gracious to her husband's friends and enemies alike. She was so well loved that even her use of snuff and rumors that she wore cosmetics didn't harm her reputation.

Dolley Madison is best remembered today for saving invaluable documents and a portrait of George Washington minutes before the British captured and burned the new capital in 1814. Her actions at this time illustrate her courage and determination.

Back in Virginia after James Madison's retirement, Dolley continued to entertain grandly until her husband's death in 1836. Soon afterward, she returned to Washington, though her finances were depleted by the gambling debts of her son. Congress purchased James Madison's papers and thereby helped to provide Dolley a modest income. Dolley Madison's home was once again the center of social life in Washington, and she enjoyed the love of all who knew her until her death in 1849 at the age of eighty-one.

Elizabeth Kortright Monroe

Served as First Lady during the term of her husband, James Monroe, fifth President of the United States

BORN	June 30, 1768
PLACE OF BIRTH	New York, New York
ANCESTRY	Dutch, English
MOTHER	Hannah Aspinwall Kortright
FATHER	Laurence Kortright
HUSBAND	James Monroe (1758-1831)
CHILDREN	Three: 1 boy, 2 girls
EDUCATION	Educated at home
AGE AT INAUGURATION	48
YEARS AS FIRST LADY	1817-1825
DIED	September 23, 1830
CAUSE OF DEATH	Rheumatic heart disease

Born into a prosperous New York family in 1768, Elizabeth Kortright was a graceful, handsome, and self-confident young woman. In 1786 she married James Monroe, who was a young and ambitious Virginia lawyer. The couple had two daughters and a son. The son died at the age of two. Senator, Governor of Virginia, Minister to France and to England, James Monroe was politically successful, and his wife soon moved in the highest social circles of both the United States and Europe.

Elizabeth particularly loved France, and France loved her too. She is credited with helping to free Lafayette's wife from prison. Elizabeth enjoyed the artistic and literary life of Paris and felt much at home in continental circles. Many people in Washington looked forward to having a First Lady who had spent ten years in society abroad—what entertaining parties she would throw!

But when Elizabeth Monroe arrived in Washington, it was soon clear that she would not reign as social queen. She did not hold open houses, preferring to entertain only on special occasions. She neglected to call on the wives of diplomats and Congressmen. She avoided White House dinners, and the absence of a hostess meant that other wives had to stay home too. She was away from Washington for months at a time, visiting her married daughters. Elizabeth's refusal to do what Washington society expected of her caused widespread resentment. Although she suffered from rheumatoid arthritis and poor health, many residents of Washington did not understand why Mrs. Monroe refrained from lavish entertaining.

Elizabeth Kortright Monroe was an elegant and regal woman who preferred privacy to public appearances. This proved disappointing to those who were accustomed to the gay socializing of Dolley Madison, the previous First Lady. At the end of President Monroe's two terms in office, Elizabeth Monroe was still a stranger to many.

But on formal occasions, Elizabeth would shine. Her dresses were ordered from France. She was gracious and poised and retained her youthful beauty. Eventually the American people accepted the First Lady's ways, and both President and Mrs. Monroe left the White House amid general good will. They retired to Virginia, where Elizabeth died in 1830 at the age of sixty-three.

Louisa Catherine Johnson Adams

Served as First Lady during the term of her husband, John Quincy Adams, sixth President of the United States

BORN   February 12, 1775
PLACE OF BIRTH   London, England
ANCESTRY   English
MOTHER   Catherine Nuth Johnson
FATHER   Joshua Johnson
HUSBAND   John Quincy Adams (1767-1848)
CHILDREN   Four: 3 boys, 1 girl
EDUCATION   Private tutors
AGE AT INAUGURATION   50
YEARS AS FIRST LADY   1825-1829
DIED   May 15, 1852
CAUSE OF DEATH   Natural causes

Louisa Catherine Johnson was born in London in 1775 to an English mother and an American father. She was educated in France and was thoroughly French in her manner and dress. Back in London, surrounded by English tutors and governesses, she studied music and literature. When John Quincy Adams met her, the nineteen-year-old Louisa was quite a catch—bright, pretty, educated, and wealthy. The two were married three years later, in 1797, and settled in Berlin where John was United States Minister.

In Berlin, Louisa began to suffer from the ailments and depression that would plague her all her life. John was absorbed in his work and Louisa felt lonely and neglected. Things did not improve when the couple moved to the United States. Louisa, who had never been to America, found everything very strange. She liked living in Washington when John became a Senator, but she was often alone with their three sons. Soon John was appointed U.S. Minister to Russia. Louisa was stunned to learn that he planned to leave their oldest sons with his parents and take just her and their youngest son with him.

Life in St. Petersburg was hard. Winters were cold, money was scarce, and Louisa's health suffered. She missed her sons, and gave birth to a baby girl who lived only a year. But Louisa kept up with the socializing expected of a diplomat's wife. While John was in Paris on business, he instructed Louisa by letter to dispose of their property in Russia and meet him in Paris. This was an immense job, ending with a grueling and dangerous forty-day coach trip across war-torn Europe.

John Adams became President Monroe's Secretary of State in 1817, and the family returned to Washington. Louisa began entertaining and calling on other political wives, creating an aura of popularity around her husband. She dreaded living in the White House, but she worked hard to help her husband get elected President. His term was a difficult one for the couple, and although Louisa was a gracious and dutiful First Lady, she was not a happy one, and John was an unpopular President. He grew disappointed, and Louisa was often depressed and ill. The couple preferred to stay quietly at home.

After the Presidency, John Adams spent seventeen years in the House of Representatives. These were successful and happy years for him and Louisa. Together they got involved in the anti-slavery and the women's rights movements. John died in the Speaker's Room of the House in 1848. Louisa had a stroke in 1849 that left her partially paralyzed. She died four years later at the age of seventy-seven.

Emily Tennessee Donelson

Served as First Lady during the term of her uncle, Andrew Jackson, seventh President of the United States

BORN	1808
PLACE OF BIRTH	Tennessee
ANCESTRY	British
MOTHER	Unknown
FATHER	Unknown
HUSBAND	Andrew Jackson Donelson
CHILDREN	Four
EDUCATION	Old Academy School in Nashville
AGE AT INAUGURATION	21
YEARS AS FIRST LADY	1829-1836
DIED	December 20, 1836
CAUSE OF DEATH	Tuberculosis

Rachel Jackson died of a heart attack a few months before her husband's inauguration. Just before she died, she asked that her nephew's wife take her place as official hostess. Emily Donelson, a sweet but unsophisticated young woman, suddenly found herself lady of the White House.

Rachel Jackson had not been happy contemplating the move to Washington when her husband became President. Hoping to make his wife more comfortable, President Jackson planned to bring Emily and her husband Andrew to the White House. Andrew became the President's private secretary. Emily had never traveled far from her native Tennessee and she'd had little education, but she rose to the task of being the President's hostess. White House visitors were soon praising Emily's pleasant, simple ways, and her dinner parties were splendid affairs.

Emily gave birth to four children in the White House. Between the Donelson children and numerous visiting relatives, the Executive Mansion was bursting. The President loved the happy sound of children and could often be found holding a sleeping baby or playing with a toddler. Then Emily, who had been frail all of her life, became ill with tuberculosis. She left the White House and returned to Tennessee in 1836, where she died several months later.

Angelica Singleton Van Buren

Served as First Lady during the term of her father-in-law, Martin Van Buren, eighth President of the United States

BORN	1816
PLACE OF BIRTH	South Carolina
ANCESTRY	British
MOTHER	Mary Coles Singleton
FATHER	Richard Singleton
HUSBAND	Abraham Van Buren (1807-1873)
CHILDREN	Two: 1 boy, 1 girl
EDUCATION	Madame Grelaud's Seminary in Philadelphia
AGE AT INAUGURATION	23
YEARS AS FIRST LADY	1839-1841
DIED	1878
CAUSE OF DEATH	Natural causes

Dolley Madison, still the queen of Washington society, realized that a woman was badly needed in the White House when President Van Buren moved in with his four bachelor sons. Many people in Washington were dismayed that the social hub of the nation was in the hands of five unmarried men. The atmosphere of the Executive Mansion was somewhat dull and austere. Simple dinners were the only entertainment.

The indomitable Dolley introduced young Angelica Singleton, a cousin visiting from South Carolina, to the President and his sons. Angelica was pretty, energetic, and had perfect manners—a sweet southern belle. Abraham, the President's oldest son was quite taken with her, and she with him. Angelica and Abraham were married in 1838.

The President was thrilled and relieved, and wasted no time installing Angelica as White House hostess. During their European "honeymoon" in 1839, Angelica met the young Queen Victoria of England. Angelica helped promote the fashion of hoop skirts, being one of the first to wear them in this country. Her attempts to infuse European customs into formal entertaining failed after the years of easy country ways in the Jackson White House. But with Dolley Madison's help, Angelica was soon giving lively parties. Everyone admired the new young woman in the White House. Although she had a girlish modesty, she was charming and vivacious, and made her guests feel at ease. Angelica and Abraham, who became his father's private secretary, lived happily in the White House. A baby girl was born there, but died soon after birth.

After the President's term ended, Angelica and her husband traveled in Europe and lived for a time in her native South Carolina. Afterwards, they made their home in New York City, where Angelica died in 1878.

Anna Tuthill Symmes Harrison

Served as First Lady during the term of her husband, William Henry Harrison, ninth President of the United States

BORN	July 25, 1775
PLACE OF BIRTH	Morristown, New Jersey
ANCESTRY	English
MOTHER	Anna Tuthill Symmes
FATHER	John Cleves Symmes
HUSBAND	William Henry Harrison (1773-1841)
CHILDREN	Ten: 6 boys, 4 girls
EDUCATION	Boarding school, New York, New York
AGE AT INAUGURATION	65
YEARS AS FIRST LADY	One month, 1841
DIED	February 25, 1864
CAUSE OF DEATH	Natural causes

Anna Tuthill Symmes was born in New Jersey in 1775. Her mother died soon after her birth. When Anna was four her father brought her to Long Island to be cared for by her grandparents. Anna went to boarding school in New York City; she was the first President's wife to have a formal education.

When Anna was nineteen, her father was appointed to be a territorial judge and governor in Ohio. Her father had remarried, and Anna settled into frontier life. There she met and promptly fell in love with Captain William Henry Harrison. Anna's father did not approve of the match, but young Anna and William were married by a justice of the peace while her father was away.

Anna was a hard-working woman, and the Harrisons' farm thrived. The couple had ten children, and Anna educated them herself. She was very active in her church, and her home was always open to friends and strangers alike.

Anna was proud of her husband's accomplishments. He was a commander during the War of 1812, a Governor, a Congressman, then a Senator. However, she did not support his bid for the Presidency. The Washington world of politics, society, and fashion did not appeal to her. She preferred that her husband stay home and cultivate his farm. After all, he was sixty-eight years old, and Anna was sixty-five. But Harrison won the election. Anna, who had been ill, chose to follow the advice of her doctor. She waited for milder weather to make the trip to Washington. Her widowed daughter-in-law, Jane Harrison, went in her place.

President William Henry Harrison caught a cold on the day of his inauguration and died of pneumonia thirty days later. His was the shortest term of any American President. Anna Harrison, the First Lady, had not arrived in Washington yet. Anna did not remarry, living most of the rest of her life in North Bend. The last few years she stayed with her only surviving son, John Scott, father of Benjamin Harrison, who became the twenty-third president of the United States. She died in 1864 at the age of eighty-eight.

Priscilla Cooper Tyler

Served as First Lady during the term of her father-in-law, John Tyler, tenth President of the United States

BORN   June 14, 1816
PLACE OF BIRTH   New York, New York
ANCESTRY   British
MOTHER   Mary Fairlee Cooper (1790-1833)
FATHER   Thomas A. Cooper (?-1849)
HUSBAND   Robert Tyler (1816-1877)
CHILDREN   Nine
EDUCATION   Studied with her father to become an actress
AGE AT INAUGURATION   26
YEARS AS FIRST LADY   1841-1844
DIED   December 29, 1889
CAUSE OF DEATH   Natural causes

Priscilla Cooper, born in New York, grew up happily in Pennsylvania. She was devoted to her father, who was an actor. When he encouraged her to join him on stage, Priscilla was happy to oblige him. To the dismay of the rest of the family, father and daughter traveled around the country together for five years, acting in plays and getting favorable reviews.

Perhaps the best review came from young Robert Tyler, who saw Priscilla perform in *Othello* and fell in love with her instantly. Priscilla had been longing for the security of marriage, and she and Robert were married in 1839.

When Robert's father, John Tyler, ran for Vice President on the Harrison ticket, Priscilla wrote everyone she knew to gather support for her father-in-law. Harrison won his bid for the Presidency but died soon afterward, making John Tyler the new President. Since Tyler's wife Letitia was an invalid, he asked Priscilla to serve as First Lady.

When Priscilla Tyler arrived in Washington to take on the job of White House hostess, many people knew her as a stage actress. In 1841, acting was not considered a respectable pursuit for a young lady, but Priscilla's beauty, poise, and charm won the hearts of all who visited the White House.

Priscilla, always full of fun and adventure, was thrilled with the White House. She gave many parties and dinners, both formal and informal, and was constantly entertaining guests. Her natural friendliness and occasional advice from Dolley Madison guaranteed that Priscilla's parties were successful.

Although she was often exhausted from endless entertaining, Priscilla was sad to leave the White House in 1844. But President Tyler, a widower since 1842, had just remarried and there was a new First Lady, Julia Gardiner Tyler for the remainder of his term. Priscilla and her family settled in Montgomery, Alabama. She remained a much-loved and respected person until her death in 1889.

Sarah Childress Polk

Served as First lady during the term of her husband, James Knox Polk, eleventh President of the United States

BORN	September 4, 1803
PLACE OF BIRTH	Rutherford County, Tennessee
ANCESTRY	Scots-Irish
MOTHER	Elizabeth Whitsitt Childress
FATHER	Joel Childress
HUSBAND	James Knox Polk (1795-1849)
CHILDREN	None
EDUCATION	Moravian Female Academy, Salem, North Carolina
AGE AT INAUGURATION	41
YEARS AS FIRST LADY	1845-1849
DIED	August 14, 1891
CAUSE OF DEATH	Natural causes

Sarah Childress, born on a Tennessee plantation, enjoyed a happy childhood and an excellent education. She met James Polk in 1821. It is said that she agreed to marry him only if he ran for the state legislature. He ran and won, and the two were married in 1824. Polk ran for Congress later that year, and Sarah eagerly accompanied him to Washington.

Sarah loved the Capital. She enjoyed mingling in Washington society, and she accompanied her husband everywhere. Domestic chores did not interest her, and the couple never had children. Sarah was free to join in her husband's career. When Polk ran for Governor of Tennessee, Sarah worked hard for his election and was quite a success as the Governor's wife.

As First Lady, Sarah continued to work side by side with her husband. She scanned books and papers for material and ideas that might interest him, she discussed political issues, she kept him informed when he was out of town. Yet publicly she was careful to stay in the bounds of accepted feminine behavior, and she won many friends with her charm and intelligence. A strict Presbyterian, Sarah banned cards, liquor, and dancing at the White House. Her parties were austere affairs, for she felt strongly that dancing and frivolity were disrespectful to the office of the Presidency.

At White House receptions, Sarah was more likely to be found discussing politics with the gentlemen than making small talk with the ladies. Her friends in Washington were important men and outspoken women, and the First Lady had admirers even among the President's political foes.

James Polk died in 1849, just a few months after leaving office. Sarah made their retirement home in Nashville into a museum dedicated to her husband. She lived there for forty-two years and received many visitors. During the Civil War she entertained both Confederate and Union officers. Sarah died in 1891, just before her eighty-eighth birthday.

Mary Elizabeth Taylor Bliss Dandridge

Served as First Lady during the term of her father, Zachary Taylor, twelfth President of the United States

BORN	April 20, 1824
PLACE OF BIRTH	Jefferson County, Kentucky
ANCESTRY	English
MOTHER	Margaret Mackall Smith Taylor (1788-1852)
FATHER	Zachary Taylor (1784-1850)
HUSBANDS	William Wallace Smith Bliss (1815-1853)
	Philip Pendleton Dandridge
CHILDREN	None
EDUCATION	Finishing school in Philadelphia, Pennsylvania
AGE AT INAUGURATION	24
YEARS AS FIRST LADY	1849-1850
DIED	July 26, 1909
CAUSE OF DEATH	Natural causes

Betty Taylor helped her mother make rough frontier homes comfortable, as her father, Zachary Taylor built his successful army career moving from one military outpost to another. After attending a boarding school in Philadelphia, Betty met Captain William Bliss, who served in the army under General Taylor and was one of his favorites. The whole Taylor family was impressed with Captain Bliss, and Betty married him in 1848.

When Zachary Taylor was nominated for President, his wife Margaret complained that it was a plot to deprive her of his attention. She followed him to Washington after he won the election, but stoutly refused to take part in Washington society and had no intention of assuming the role of First Lady. Betty and her new husband accompanied the family to Washington. Margaret Taylor stayed upstairs in her room, seeing just relatives and close friends and leaving the White House only to attend church. She asked her daughter, Betty Bliss, to assume the responsibilities of First Lady.

Betty served as hostess and held not only state dinners, but dances for young people as well. She capably handled domestic details and was a popular hostess—Washington had developed a fondness for sweet, girlish First Ladies. As was often the case with husbands of surrogate First Ladies, Captain Bliss became Taylor's private secretary.

President Taylor died suddenly in 1850. Betty, her husband, and her mother moved to Louisiana, where Margaret Taylor died four years later. After Bliss died, Betty married Philip Dandridge. She died in 1909 at the age of eighty-five.

Abigail Powers Fillmore

Served as First Lady during the term of her husband, Millard Fillmore, thirteenth President of the United States

BORN   March 13, 1798
PLACE OF BIRTH   Stillwater, New York
ANCESTRY   English
MOTHER   Abigail Newland Powers
FATHER   Lemuel Powers
HUSBAND   Millard Fillmore (1800-1874)
CHILDREN   Two: 1 boy, 1 girl
EDUCATION   Early schooling uncertain; became a teacher
AGE AT INAUGURATION   52
YEARS AS FIRST LADY   1850-1853
DIED   March 30, 1853
CAUSE OF DEATH   Pneumonia

Abigail's father died soon after she was born, and her mother took young Abigail and her brother to a frontier community in western New York. Abigail, who loved books and read everything she could, became a schoolteacher. One day in 1818, when she was nineteen, an eighteen-year-old farm boy joined her class. His name was Millard Fillmore, and he wanted to become a lawyer. Abigail and her bright new student were engaged within a year.

The engagement lasted eight years while Millard struggled to become a lawyer. Abigail continued to teach, even after they were married in 1826. Millard won election to the New York legislature, and in 1832 was elected to the U.S. House of Representatives. The couple had two children. Abigail was no longer teaching, but she was still learning. She studied French and piano, and her husband never returned from a trip without an armful of new books for their growing library.

Fillmore became Vice President in 1849. Sixteen months later, President Taylor died and Millard and Abigail Fillmore moved into the White House. Social life in the White House was subdued following Taylor's death and remained so for the rest of the term.

When she became First Lady, Abigail Fillmore was dismayed to find that the White House had no library. She prompted her husband to ask Congress for money for books, and proceeded to make a large room into the first White House library. Here, with her piano and harp, Abigail spent many pleasant hours.

Abigail always preferred her books and her music over Washington social life. Although she was happy to perform her role as White House hostess, private gatherings in her library were more her style. Abigail's health was failing during her husband's last months in office, and their daughter, Abby, took over many of the First Lady's social duties.

While attending the inauguration of President Pierce, Abigail caught a cold and died of pneumonia a few months later. Newspapers featured stories of Abigail's sudden death, and government and public offices closed in official mourning.

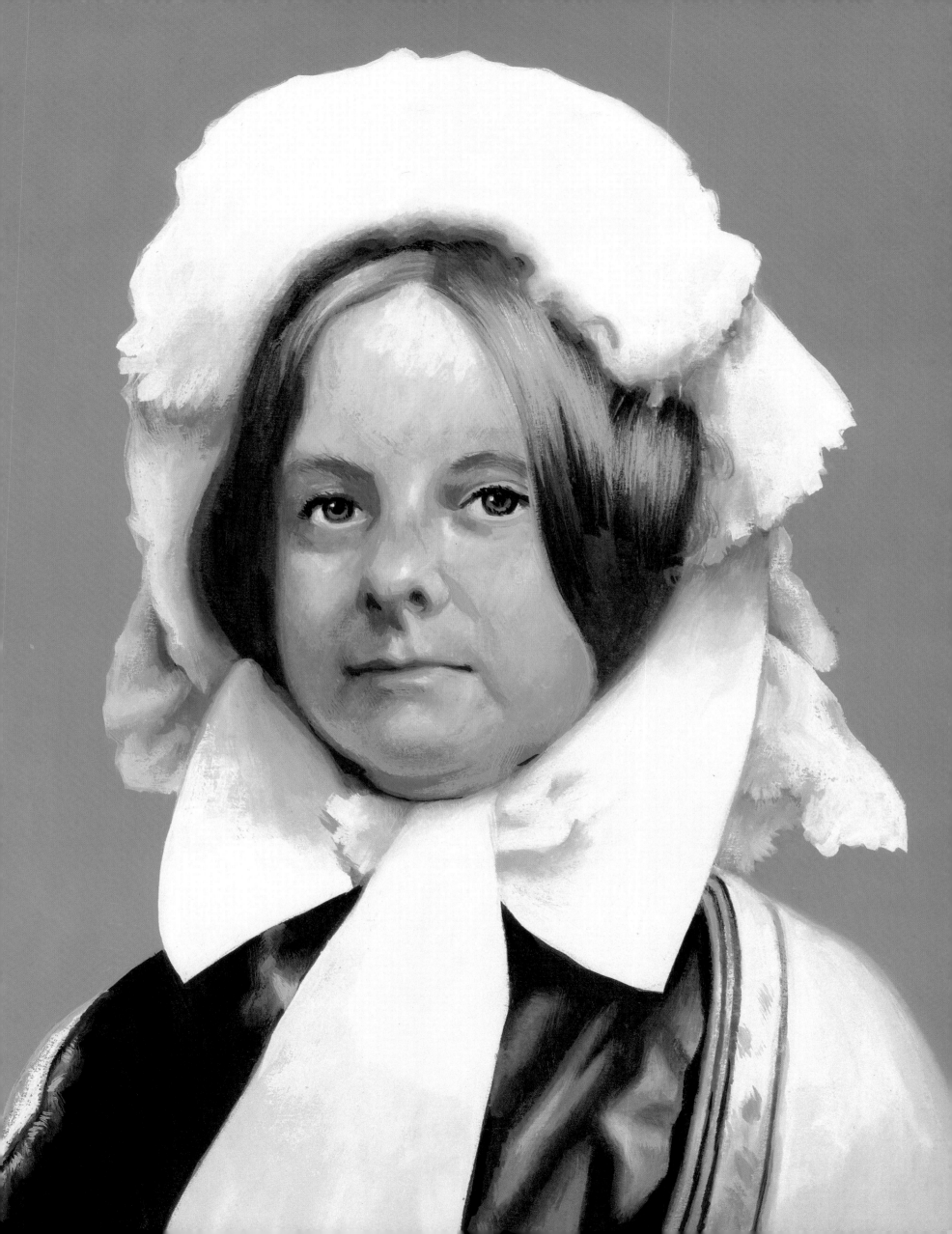

Jane Means Appleton Pierce

Served as First Lady during the term of her husband, Franklin Pierce, fourteenth President of the United States

BORN	March 12, 1806
PLACE OF BIRTH	Hampton, New Hampshire
ANCESTRY	British
MOTHER	Elizabeth Appleton
FATHER	Jesse Appleton (?-1819)
HUSBAND	Franklin Pierce (1804-1869)
CHILDREN	Three boys
EDUCATION	Well educated as daughter of Bowdoin College president
AGE AT INAUGURATION	46
YEARS AS FIRST LADY	1853-1857
DIED	December 2, 1863
CAUSE OF DEATH	Tuberculosis

Jane Appleton's father died when she was thirteen, and she and her mother moved to Amherst, Massachusetts. There Jane met Franklin Pierce, a young lawyer, and the two were soon engaged. Jane's family took a dim view of politics and disapproved of Franklin's political ambitions; besides, he was known to drink. But, in 1834, Jane married him.

Jane was shy and melancholy, and always in delicate health. She was too frail for household chores, so her husband hired a couple to live with them, cook meals, and take care of the house. Jane had three sons, but none lived to adulthood. Jane's first child died in infancy; the second died at age four. Franklin and Jane were devoted to their third son, Bennie. Pierce, who had been a Congressman and a Senator, returned from Washington to resume his law career, and Jane thought with relief that his public life was over.

Jane never wanted her husband to be in politics. She fainted at the news that he had been nominated to be President. But Jane was fiercely religious, and could only bow to God's will when her husband became President of the United States.

On a family train trip from Massachusetts to New Hampshire two months before Franklin Pierce's inauguration, the train derailed and eleven-year-old Bennie was killed. Jane never recovered from her shock and grief. The inauguration took place, but without an inaugural ball and without Jane. She eventually joined her husband at the White House but stayed upstairs most of the time, succumbing completely to grief and illness and finding her only solace in prayer.

Varina Davis, wife of Secretary of War Jefferson Davis, occasionally served as official hostess. Visits from Varina and her little boy and her awareness of Varina's success as hostess may have prompted Jane to try harder to fulfill her political role. Eventually she began making public appearances at dinners and receptions, but she seemed ghostly and sad. The White House was indeed a bleak place.

At the end of Franklin Pierce's term, he took his wife abroad to try to restore her health. But Jane, always carrying Bennie's Bible and a lock of his hair, returned home little improved. She died in Massachusetts in 1863.

Harriet Lane Johnston

Served as First Lady during the term of her uncle, James Buchanan, fifteenth President of the United States

BORN	May 9, 1830
PLACE OF BIRTH	Mercersburg, Pennsylvania
ANCESTRY	English, Scotch, Irish
MOTHER	Jane Buchanan Lane (1793-1839)
FATHER	Elliot Tole Lane (1784-1840)
HUSBAND	Henry Elliott Johnston
CHILDREN	Two boys
EDUCATION	Visitation Convent, Georgetown, Washington, D.C.
AGE AT INAUGURATION	26
YEARS AS FIRST LADY	1857-1861
DIED	1906
CAUSE OF DEATH	Heart failure

By the time Harriet Lane was ten years old, both her parents had died and she was the ward of her uncle, James Buchanan. Buchanan was a Senator in Washington, and he sent Harriet to the best school in the city. Later, Harriet visited the White House when her uncle served in President Polk's cabinet. She accompanied her uncle to London when he was envoy to Great Britain. When Buchanan became President in 1857, Harriet was already well-known in political circles and fashionable society.

Harriet acted as First Lady for Buchanan, the only bachelor President. She was very popular. The press called her the "Democratic Queen." Women imitated her style of dress, and she charmed everyone with her enthusiasm and poise. Even with the possibility of Civil War on everyone's mind, the White House was merrier than it had been in years.

Harriet had a serious side as well. At a time of internal conflict in the country, she used diplomacy and tact when arranging the seating at state dinners. She invited artists to White House affairs to expose the politicians to the value of culture. American Indians came to her for assistance and expressed their gratitude by making "Harriet" a popular Indian name. Harriet demonstrated enough knowledge of politics to become the President's confidante.

During her tenure at the White House, the Prince of Wales (later King Edward VII) was a guest. This was the first visit by a member of the royal family to the United States. On another occasion, she was hostess at a reception honoring the first Japanese diplomatic mission to the U.S.

Five years after leaving the White House, Harriet married Henry Johnston, a banker from Baltimore. The couple had two sons. When she died in 1906, Harriet bequeathed half of her sizeable art collection to the government. This donation was the basis for the National Gallery of Art. The rest of her collection was left to the Johns Hopkins Hospital in Baltimore. She also donated a generous sum of money to the pediatric division of the Johns Hopkins Hospital, where the Harriet Lane Outpatient Clinics still serve thousands of children.

Mary Ann Todd Lincoln

Served as First Lady during the term of her husband, Abraham Lincoln, sixteenth President of the United States

BORN	December 13, 1818
PLACE OF BIRTH	Lexington, Kentucky
ANCESTRY	English
MOTHER	Eliza Ann Parker Todd (1794-1825)
FATHER	Robert Smith Todd (1791-1865)
HUSBAND	Abraham Lincoln (1809-1865)
CHILDREN	Four boys
EDUCATION	Mme. Montelle's School, Lexington, Kentucky
AGE AT INAUGURATION	43
YEARS AS FIRST LADY	1861-1865
DIED	July 16, 1882
CAUSE OF DEATH	Stroke

Born into a prosperous Kentucky family in 1818, Mary Ann Todd went to all the best schools. She was an excellent student but a prankster as well, witty but sarcastic and outspoken, charming but short-tempered and impulsive. At age twenty, Mary went to live with her sister in Springfield, Illinois. There she met Abraham Lincoln, and after a stormy courtship they were married in 1842. Lincoln built a successful law practice, and he and Mary had four sons, one of whom died at the age of four.

No one was happier than Mary when Lincoln became President, and she was eager to help make her husband's term a success. She redecorated the somewhat shabby White House, gave elegant parties, and dressed in exquisite taste. But Mary's efforts worked against her. The Civil War had begun and her dinners and fine clothes seemed callous and extravagant. Worse still, she was from a border state and had relatives fighting for the Confederacy. Ill-founded rumors spread that Mary was a traitor.

Mary's experience as First Lady was not what she had expected. Gay and ambitious, she loved attention and looked forward to being the belle of Washington. But it seemed that Mrs. Lincoln could do nothing right. Throughout her stay in the White House, she was criticized and frustrated.

In 1862, Mary's eleven-year old son Willie died of typhoid fever. The Lincolns were shattered by the loss, and Mary came close to total collapse. But when she bought costly mourning clothes and special mourning jewelry, the public was outraged. Mary's reputation grew steadily worse. Stories were told that the First Lady threw tantrums when a hat she wanted was not available, when her purchases were not delivered on time, or when a dress was not quite what she expected. In addition, she was said to be manipulative, jealous, and selfish. But Mary never bothered to defend herself, never retreated to an upstairs room as some of her predecessors had done. Always proud and determined, she chose to stay in the limelight.

Lincoln's assassination in 1865 ended Mary's ordeal as First Lady, but her troubles were far from over. Although she was able to pay her debts with her husband's estate, she became obsessed with a fear of poverty. Her son Tad died in 1871, and her reckless spending continued. Her only remaining son Robert, fearing that she would squander all her money, had her declared incompetent. When Mary was put in Robert's care, he committed her to an institution that specialized in caring for mentally troubled women from the upper class. After three months, her sister had her released and declared competent again.

Suffering from cataracts, arthritis, and other health problems, Mary visited France but returned increasingly plagued by anxieties and fear of poverty. She went to her sister's house, broken and ill, and died there at the age of sixty-four.

Eliza McCardle Johnson

Served as First Lady during the term of her husband, Andrew Johnson, seventeenth President of the United States

BORN	October 4, 1810
PLACE OF BIRTH	Leesburg, Tennessee
ANCESTRY	Scotch
MOTHER	Sarah Phillips McCardle
FATHER	John McCardle
HUSBAND	Andrew Johnson (1808-1875)
CHILDREN	Five: 3 boys, 2 girls
EDUCATION	Rhea Academy, Greeneville, Tennessee
AGE AT INAUGURATION	54
YEARS AS FIRST LADY	1865-1869
DIED	January 15, 1876
CAUSE OF DEATH	Tuberculosis

Eliza McCardle was sixteen years old when Andrew Johnson, only seventeen, opened a tailor shop in her hometown of Greeneville, Tennessee. The two were married within a year. Eliza taught Andrew reading, writing and arithmetic, since she had gone to school and he had not. She was also proficient at running a household and raising their five children on a limited income. But Johnson soon prospered in both business and politics. President Lincoln appointed him military governor of Tennessee in Nashville in 1862.

Eliza remained in Greeneville with her youngest son while the Civil War raged around them. East Tennessee, loyal to the Union, was soon under martial law, and Unionists like the Johnsons were forced to leave. Eliza got permission to cross Confederate lines to join her husband in Nashville. She made a grueling journey that left her exhausted and seriously ill with tuberculosis. The loss of a son and son-in-law in the war weakened her further. Eliza stayed in Nashville when her husband became Lincoln's Vice President, but she traveled to Washington as First Lady a month later when Lincoln was assassinated.

Two sons, two daughters, a son-in-law, and five grandchildren moved to the White House with her. While she lived at the White House, Eliza spent most of her time in a room on the second floor. Social duties were carried out by elder daughter Martha Patterson.

Ill and weak, she refused invitations and requests for interviews. President Johnson's impeachment trial was an added burden for her. In 1866, she made a formal appearance at a reception for Queen Emma, widow of King Kamehameha IV of the Sandwich (Hawaiian) Islands. She also made a public appearance in 1867 at a birthday party for her husband.

Eliza was relieved to return to Tennessee at the end of her husband's term. They moved back into their restored house in Greeneville, where Eliza died in 1876.

Julia Boggs Dent Grant

Served as First Lady during the term of her husband, Ulysses S. Grant, eighteenth President of the United States

BORN	January 26, 1826
PLACE OF BIRTH	White Haven, St. Louis, Missouri
ANCESTRY	English
MOTHER	Ellen Wrenshall Dent (1795-1857)
FATHER	Frederick Dent (1795-1873)
HUSBAND	Ulysses S. Grant (1822-1885)
CHILDREN	Four: 3 boys, 1 girl
EDUCATION	Boarding school in St. Louis, Missouri
AGE AT INAUGURATION	43
YEARS AS FIRST LADY	1869-1877
DIED	December 14, 1902
CAUSE OF DEATH	Bronchitis, kidney and heart disease

Julia Boggs Dent grew up on a plantation near St. Louis, enjoying the life of a young Southern belle. She was cross-eyed and plain, but popular nonetheless. Lieutenant Ulysses Grant fell in love with her. Julia and "Ulys" were married in 1848 in St. Louis. Julia's family gave them 60 acres of land and three slaves. Ulysses' family refused to attend the wedding because the Dents were slave owners.

Julia always believed that her husband was destined for greatness. When he became a general during the Civil War, she followed him proudly to his headquarters. Like Martha Washington, she tended the sick and wounded soldiers and helped keep up everyone's morale.

Although Julia was a kind and simple woman, she was not a stranger to fashion. When her husband was elected President, she held dinners, receptions, and open houses, and her parties were both elegant and merry. After the strain of the Civil War, the public was overjoyed at the return of gaiety and finery to the White House. Young Nellie Grant's White House wedding was a splendid affair that was the talk of Washington.

Julia had political opinions as well, and she didn't hesitate to share them with her husband. The President teased her that he had to hide his list of Cabinet appointments to keep her from arguing with his choices. Julia enjoyed being First Lady, the nation's premier hostess and confidante to the President. She was sorely disappointed when her husband was not nominated for a third term.

After leaving the White House, the Grants took a trip around the world. For the next two and a half years, they visited famous people and places the world over and were treated royally everywhere they went. Back home in the United States, they settled in New York, and Ulysses began writing his memoirs, in part to support the family following a private business failure. After his death, the royalties from this book provided Julia with the means for a comfortable life. She traveled and enjoyed friendships with women's suffragist Susan B. Anthony and with Jefferson Davis's widow Varina. She died at the age of seventy-six in 1902.

Lucy Ware Webb Hayes

Served as First Lady during the term of her husband, Rutherford B. Hayes, nineteenth President of the United States

BORN	August 28, 1831
PLACE OF BIRTH	Chillicothe, Ohio
ANCESTRY	English
MOTHER	Maria Cook Webb (1801-1866)
FATHER	James Webb (?-1833)
HUSBAND	Rutherford Birchard Hayes (1822-1893)
CHILDREN	Eight: 7 boys, 1 girl
EDUCATION	Ohio Wesleyan Female College, Cincinnati, Ohio
AGE AT INAUGURATION	45
YEARS AS FIRST LADY	1877-1881
DIED	June 25, 1889
CAUSE OF DEATH	Stroke

Lucy Webb grew up in a family that actively supported the reforms of the time: abolition, women's rights, religious and educational reforms. Lucy's father died when she was two years old. Mrs. Webb moved with her children to several Ohio towns to give her sons the best available education. Lucy benefited as well. She attended good schools along with her brothers, and graduated from Ohio Wesleyan Female College in Cincinnati.

Bright and well-informed, young Lucy was a staunch Methodist and was enthusiastic about social reform, particularly women's rights. She met Rutherford Hayes, a Cincinnati lawyer, in 1847, and they were married in 1852. Lucy continued her interest in social causes and was probably influential in her husband's switch from the Whig to the antislavery Republican party.

During the Civil War, she often visited her husband and his troops. She was well liked by the soldiers and developed a lifelong interest in the welfare of veterans and the orphaned children of soldiers. Lucy and Rutherford had eight children, but three died in infancy.

When Lucy became First Lady in 1877, it was clear that she was not the frivolous type. She dressed simply, didn't fuss with her hair, and didn't powder her face. She displayed a sober and quiet dignity. In addition, she was the first President's wife to have a college degree. Many people thought Lucy would represent the New Woman: an intellectual woman with political opinions. But Lucy didn't get involved in politics. She did begin a tradition that continues today—the annual Easter Egg Roll on the White House lawn.

In the White House, there were daily prayer meetings, Bible readings, and Sunday evening hymns. The food at state dinners was delicious, but alcohol was never served. Though the liquor ban was the President's idea, the First Lady was thought to be responsible and was given the nickname "Lemonade Lucy." The "dry" White House indirectly supported the growing Women's Christian Temperance Union.

The Hayeses retired to Fremont, Ohio, at the end of the Presidential term. Lucy busied herself with church activities until she died of a stroke in 1889.

Lucretia Rudolph Garfield

Served as First Lady during the term of her husband, James A. Garfield, twentieth President of the United States

BORN	April 19, 1832
PLACE OF BIRTH	Hiram, Ohio
ANCESTRY	German
MOTHER	Arabella Green Mason Rudolph (1810-1879)
FATHER	Zebulon Rudolph (1803-1897)
HUSBAND	James Abram Garfield (1831-1881)
CHILDREN	Seven: 5 boys, 2 girls
EDUCATION	Geauga Seminary and Western Reserve Eclectic Institute (later Hiram College), Hiram, Ohio
AGE AT INAUGURATION	48
YEARS AS FIRST LADY	1881
DIED	March 14, 1918
CAUSE OF DEATH	Natural causes

Lucretia Rudolph and James Garfield had much in common. They were classmates in a religious school in Hiram, Ohio, and each had a serious outlook on life. They were disciplined, diligent, and shared a love for art and literature. But James's outgoing nature clashed with Lucretia's shyness and reserve. Their courtship was a long and troubled one, and when they were finally married in 1858, they both had doubts.

The newlyweds set up housekeeping in Hiram, but the Civil War brought about long separations early in their marriage. Despite a stormy start and some indiscretions on James's part, their relationship settled down. They had seven children, two of whom died in infancy.

While still in the army, James Garfield was elected to Congress in 1862. When his family joined him in Washington, Lucretia was overjoyed by the attention her husband gave her and their children. James became more domesticated, Lucretia more outgoing. They read to each other, attended meetings of Washington's Literary Society together, made social calls, and dined out.

James Garfield became President in 1881. Lucretia was ill with malaria for her first few months as First Lady, and went to a seaside resort to recover. Less than four months after his inauguration, James Garfield was shot. Desperate and weak, Lucretia rushed back to Washington to nurse her husband. He died three months later.

With the support of a Congressional pension, Lucretia lived another thirty-six years. She traveled, read, wrote, and carefully preserved her husband's records until her death in 1918 at the age of eighty-five.

Mary Arthur McElroy

Served as First Lady during the term of her brother, Chester A. Arthur, twenty-first President of the United States

BORN	June 5, 1841
PLACE OF BIRTH	Greenwich, New York
ANCESTRY	English, Scotch, Irish
MOTHER	Malvina Stone Arthur (1802-1869)
FATHER	William Arthur (1796-1875)
HUSBAND	John McElroy
CHILDREN	Four
EDUCATION	Emma Willard's Female Seminary, Troy, New York
AGE AT INAUGURATION	40
YEARS AS FIRST LADY	1881-1885
DIED	January 8, 1917
CAUSE OF DEATH	Natural causes

Mary McElroy was asked to come to the White House and act as official hostess for her brother, Chester Arthur. Arthur's wife had died the previous year, and the President managed many of the domestic details that a First Lady would have handled. Arthur was accustomed to the finer things in life, and when he became President, he pronounced the White House unlivable. He auctioned off much of the old furniture, hired a famous designer and closely supervised the redecorating of the White House.

Mary had her own family to care for, but she happily spent several months each year serving as her brother's First Lady. She also helped Arthur with his two young children, and occasionally brought her own children to Washington to visit their uncle and cousins.

Mary became known for her warm hospitality. She made formal receptions more comfortable by treating all her guests as friends. There were many ladies at White House functions, as Mary often invited a number of women—including several former first ladies—to help her with her hostess duties. The President wanted to protect his personal life from public scrutiny, and Mary helped him maintain a strict barrier between private and official life at the White House.

Mary spent the winter social seasons in Washington and the rest of the year at home with her family. After his term as President, Chester Arthur lived with Mary's family until his death in 1886. She died in 1917.

Frances Folsom Cleveland

Served as First Lady during the terms of her husband, Grover Cleveland, twenty-second and twenty-fourth President of the United States

BORN	July 21, 1864
PLACE OF BIRTH	Buffalo, New York
ANCESTRY	British
MOTHER	Emma Cornelia Harmon Folsom
FATHER	Oscar Folsom (?-1875)
HUSBANDS	Grover Cleveland (1837-1908)
	Thomas Jex Preston, Jr. (1880-1955)
CHILDREN	Five: 2 boys, 3 girls
EDUCATION	Wells College, Aurora, New York
AGE AT INAUGURATIONS	21 and 28
YEARS AS FIRST LADY	1886-1889, 1893-1897
DIED	October 29, 1947
CAUSE OF DEATH	Natural causes

Grover Cleveland was a close friend of the Folsom family; he knew Frances as a baby and became her unofficial guardian when her father died in 1875. Cleveland bought Frances her first baby carriage and guided her through her education. By the time she was in college he was sending her flowers.

Cleveland was a bachelor when he became President in 1885, and his sister Rose acted as White House hostess. When Frances and her mother visited President Cleveland during this time, Washington gossiped that the President planned to marry Mrs. Folsom, his old friend's widow. As the months went by, it was clear that a Presidential marriage was in the air, but no one expected the bride to be twenty-two-year-old Frances!

Frances was tall and strikingly pretty, and she carried herself with such poise and authority that she seemed older than her years. She was the youngest First Lady, and her marriage in 1886 made her the first to marry a President in the White House. The marriage was a happy one, despite the twenty-seven-year age difference between husband and wife.

Washington loved young Mrs. Cleveland. Her parties were grand successes, and her beauty and charm won her many admirers. The whole country toasted the birth of a daughter in the White House. Frances was far more popular than her husband, who lost his bid for re-election. When Cleveland successfully ran for President again four years later, Frances' picture appeared on campaign posters between him and his running mate. But Frances had no interest in political issues and was content to be the wife that her husband wanted.

The Clevelands retired from public life in 1897 and settled in Princeton, where they had two sons. Grover Cleveland's health began to fail and he died in 1908. Frances, still young, married Thomas Preston in 1913. He was on the Princeton faculty, and Frances became involved in college activities and fund-raising. She died in her sleep in 1947, at the age of eighty-three.

Caroline Lavinia Scott Harrison

Served as First Lady during the term of her husband, Benjamin Harrison, twenty-third President of the United States

BORN
PLACE OF BIRTH
ANCESTRY
MOTHER
FATHER
HUSBAND
CHILDREN
EDUCATION
AGE AT INAUGURATION
YEARS AS FIRST LADY
DIED
CAUSE OF DEATH

October 1, 1832
Oxford, Ohio
English
Mary Potts Neal Scott (?-1876)
John Witherspoon Scott
Benjamin Harrison (1833-1901)
Two: 1 boy, 1 girl
Oxford Female Institute, Oxford, Ohio
56
1889-1892
October 25, 1892
Tuberculosis

Caroline Scott was born in Oxford, Ohio. Her father founded the Oxford Female Institute which Caroline attended. Her father also taught at a nearby college where young Benjamin Harrison was a student. He visited the Scott home often and fell in love with gay, artistic Caroline. The young couple married in 1853.

Harrison worked hard to build his law career, while Caroline cared for their two children and kept busy with church activities. After eight years in the Senate, Benjamin Harrison was elected President in 1889. The family that moved into the White House was large: the president, Caroline, Caroline's father, her niece, daughter, son-in-law, and three small grandchildren. Caroline's son and his family were frequent visitors as well.

The White House was not only too small for this extended family, but quite dilapidated as well. There was serious talk of building a whole new Executive Mansion, but in the end legislators voted to renovate the existing structure. Caroline was busy overseeing the massive job of modernizing, refurbishing, and refurnishing the White House. She gathered pieces of china that had been collected by previous First Ladies and assembled them into a historical display. She painted the design for the new White House china. She also painted her own decorations on White House candlesticks, vases, and flower pots, and filled the rooms with exotic plants that she grew herself.

Caroline kept herself very busy with these projects, but she was not the simple homebody that Washington socialites thought she was. She was the first president-general of the Daughters of the American Revolution. The First Lady was devoted to art and beauty. She cultivated orchids, did fine needlework, liked to paint, and was a talented pianist.

Caroline enjoyed the social life of Washington as well. Her friendliness at White House functions offset the coldness the President often displayed. She installed the first Christmas tree in the White House in 1889. She became ill in 1891 and was soon bedridden. Caroline died of tuberculosis the following year, before her husband's Presidential term was over.

Ida Saxton McKinley

Served as First Lady during the term of her husband, William McKinley, twenty-fifth President of the United States

BORN	June 8, 1847
PLACE OF BIRTH	Canton, Ohio
ANCESTRY	English
MOTHER	Catherine Dewalt Saxton
FATHER	James Asbury Saxton (1820-?)
HUSBAND	William McKinley (1843-1901)
CHILDREN	Two girls
EDUCATION	Brook Hall Seminary, Media, Pennsylvania
AGE AT INAUGURATION	49
YEAR AS FIRST LADY	1897-1901
DIED	May 26, 1907
CAUSE OF DEATH	Uncertain

Young Ida Saxton was a pretty and lively woman when she married William McKinley in 1871. She had been a Sunday School teacher in the Presbyterian Church and had worked for a time in her father's bank. The McKinleys set up housekeeping in her hometown of Canton, Ohio, and had a daughter. But several family deaths soon shattered Ida's happiness: her grandfather died, then her mother, then her second infant daughter. The birth had been difficult, and after the baby's death, Ida never recovered her health. By the time her four-year-old daughter died of typhoid fever in 1876, Ida was almost a complete invalid.

Meanwhile, William McKinley was advancing his political career. He became a Congressman, Governor of Ohio, and finally President. Ida had been an invalid for twenty years by the time she became First Lady. While many of her predecessors had used their poor health to excuse them from official duties, Ida wanted to be the center of attention. Dressed in lace and diamonds, she was too ill to do anything but sit quietly, propped up with pillows and holding flowers in her frail hands. The nature of Ida's illness was vague at the time; it was said simply that her health was "delicate." She had seizures and blinding headaches. She may have had epilepsy, which in the nineteenth century was a frightening ailment.

Only her husband knew how to deal with Ida's seizures, and he was never far from her side. He even sat next to her at state dinners, contrary to White House etiquette. When President McKinley saw a minor seizure coming, he would simply whisk a handkerchief from his pocket and place it over his wife's face, never interrupting his conversation. Ida would remove it when the seizure was over and resume talking as if nothing had happened.

Ida showed surprising strength when McKinley was shot in 1901. She bravely put on a show of health in order to encourage his recovery, but he died a week later. Ida returned to Canton, where she died in 1907, just before her sixtieth birthday.

Edith Kermit Carow Roosevelt

Served as First Lady during the term of her husband, Theodore Roosevelt, twenty-sixth President of the United States

BORN	August 6, 1861
PLACE OF BIRTH	Norwich, Connecticut
ANCESTRY	French and English
MOTHER	Gertrude Elizabeth Tyler Carow (1836-1895)
FATHER	Charles Carow (1825-1883)
HUSBAND	Theodore Roosevelt (1858-1919)
CHILDREN	Five: 4 boys, 1 girl
EDUCATION	Miss Comstock's School, New York, New York
AGE AT INAUGURATION	39
YEARS AS FIRST LADY	1901-1909
DIED	September 30, 1948
CAUSE OF DEATH	Arteriosclerosis

Edith Carow, born in Connecticut, grew up in the same privileged circles in New York City as Theodore Roosevelt. They became sweethearts, but grew apart after Roosevelt went away to Harvard. Roosevelt married Alice Hathaway Lee in 1880; her sudden death four years later left him a desolate widower with infant daughter Alice. Theodore and Edith renewed their old romance and were married in 1886.

They were an unlikely couple. She was aloof and a bit austere, while he was boyish and impetuous. But Edith liked her husband's exuberance, and Theodore appreciated her restraint. Edith and Theodore had five children together. Edith skillfully managed their large household as they moved from place to place with the advancement of Theodore's political career. Theodore Roosevelt became William McKinley's Vice President in 1901, and suddenly found himself President when McKinley was assassinated a few months later.

The Roosevelt White House was a boisterous place. There were always children and animals underfoot, including dogs, cats, guinea pigs, snakes, lizards, and rats. Newspapers gleefully reported the antics of the Roosevelt children and their pets. But while her family scrambled around her, Edith remained calm. She presided over White House parties and state dinners with confidence and dignity. Theodore's daughter by his first wife lived with them and was married at the White House in 1906.

Edith dealt swiftly with each problem she encountered. In an effort to protect her family from too much publicity, Edith and her children posed for photographs which appeared, with little information, in many popular magazines. These formal photographs preserved their privacy, satisfied public curiosity, and kept the media at bay. In addition, Edith directed White House renovations that clearly separated the family's living quarters from the offices and public rooms. She held weekly meetings with Cabinet wives to set standards for official entertaining. Edith hired caterers to handle White House parties and a secretary to handle all her correspondence.

Edith was a capable, confident woman who took a business-like approach to her duties as First Lady. The changes she instituted in White House management solved many problems both for her and her successors, and she brought a new structure to the role of First Lady.

The Roosevelts retired in 1909, but they both stayed as busy as ever. Theodore Roosevelt died ten years after his presidential term was over. Edith traveled often, did church and charity work, and kept her ties to the Republican party. Sadly, three of her four sons were killed during her widowhood. Quentin died in World War I; Theodore Jr. and Kermit died in World War II. Archie, who lived until 1979, served in both world wars. She died at the age of eighty-seven in 1948.

Helen Herron Taft

Served as First Lady during the term of her husband, William H. Taft, twenty-seventh President of the United States

BORN	June 2, 1861
PLACE OF BIRTH	Cincinnati, Ohio
ANCESTRY	English
MOTHER	Harriet Collins Herron (?-1902)
FATHER	John Williamson Herron (?-1912)
HUSBAND	William Howard Taft (1857-1930)
CHILDREN	Three: 2 boys, 1 girl
EDUCATION	University of Cincinnati, Cincinnati, Ohio
AGE AT INAUGURATION	47
YEARS AS FIRST LADY	1909-1913
DIED	May 22, 1943
CAUSE OF DEATH	Natural causes

Seventeen-year-old Helen Herron visited the White House as a guest of President Hayes, her father's old friend. She was so impressed by the Executive Mansion that she vowed to marry a man who would one day be President. And though the man she eventually married had little taste for politics, Helen got her wish.

Helen, who grew up in Cincinnati, was an outspoken and unconventional young woman. She organized meetings of young people to discuss intellectual issues. She was a schoolteacher when she met William Taft, a young lawyer, at a sledding party. They were married six years later.

William Taft was appointed a Judge the following year. He was pleased as the Supreme Court was his ambition, but Helen dreaded the stodgy, judicial life. She busied herself with their three children, took art classes, joined a book club. In 1900 William was asked to head the American civil government in the Philippines. Helen could barely wait to go. She loved adventure, and the years in the Philippines were happy ones.

Once back in the United States, William Taft got several offers from President Roosevelt for a Supreme Court appointment. Though this was the position he had always wanted, Helen opposed it. Her husband's success in the Philippines made him a likely Presidential candidate, and Helen had no intention of letting the opportunity pass. In 1908 William Taft became President, and Helen moved into the White House as the First Lady.

Helen plunged happily into her new role. She replaced some of the White House staff, rearranged the rooms, and sponsored musical performances on the White House lawn. She arranged for the planting of Washington's famous cherry trees. Two months of furious activity came to a halt when Helen suffered a severe stroke. She recovered within a year, but never resumed her vigorous pace. Nonetheless, her parties were considered to be among the most brilliant ever held in the White House.

After his term ended, William Taft had the opportunity to fulfill his fondest wish. He was appointed Chief Justice of the Supreme Court. Helen, glad to be out of the public glare, found that the judicial life now suited her. She stayed in Washington after her husband died in 1930, continuing her interest in the arts until her death in 1943.

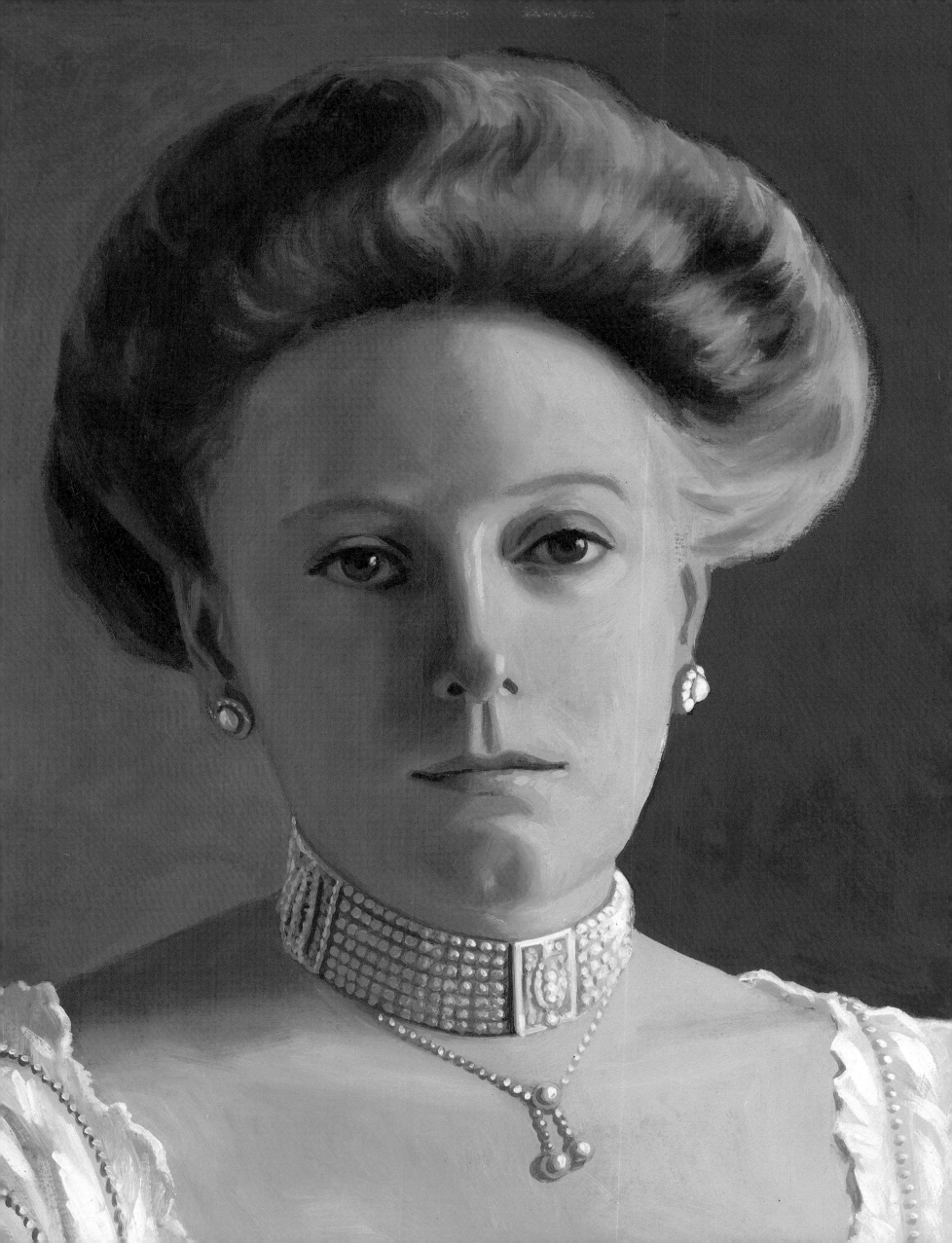

Edith Bolling Galt Wilson

Served as First Lady during the term of her husband, Woodrow Wilson, twenty-eighth President of the United States

BORN	October 15, 1872
PLACE OF BIRTH	Wytheville, Virginia
ANCESTRY	English, American Indian
MOTHER	Sallie White Bolling (1843-?)
FATHER	William Holcombe Bolling (?-1899)
HUSBANDS	Norman Galt (?-1908)
	Woodrow Wilson (1856-1924)
CHILDREN	None
EDUCATION	Martha Washington College in Abingdon, Virginia; Powell School in Richmond
AGE AT INAUGURATION	40
YEARS AS FIRST LADY	1915-1921
DIED	December 28, 1961
CAUSE OF DEATH	Natural causes

A pretty young woman from a large family, Edith Bolling married Norman Galt in 1896. The couple lived in Washington until Galt's sudden death twelve years later. One afternoon in 1915, Edith was introduced to President Wilson, who was deep in mourning after the recent death of his wife. The widow and widower soon fell in love, and were married later that year.

Some people were dismayed that the President remarried just a year after his first wife's death, but Edith was undaunted and performed her role as White House hostess with grace. She was not particularly interested in politics; her main concern was the health and happiness of her husband. And her husband rarely listened to a woman's opinion on serious issues. Nevertheless, Edith Wilson became known as the only woman to run the White House.

The entry of United States into World War I increased Edith's activities. She served food at soldiers' canteens in Washington and made clothes for the men overseas. When the war finally ended, she traveled with the President to the peace conference in Paris. Edith then accompanied her husband on his tour of the United States to promote the League of Nations. It was this trip that proved too much for the exhausted President. He collapsed with a massive stroke in the fall of 1919.

Edith now had to make a serious choice. She could insist that her husband resign his office, or agree to help him carry on his responsibilities. She was advised that resignation would be unfortunate, not only for the country but for her husband as well. He would have little incentive to recover. Yet the pressures of the Presidency would surely threaten his recovery as well. It was decided that the President would not resign. Edith became the intermediary between her husband and all diplomats, advisers, and department heads. She brought him only what she felt were the most important issues and delegated everything else.

Many people criticized this arrangement between what they called the "Presidentress and the First Man." Edith insisted that she never made any decisions regarding public policy and was interested only in her husband's health. The President did improve but was never really well again. The couple retired from public life in 1921, and Wilson died three years later.

Edith Wilson lived thirty-eight years longer and was a public figure for much of that time. She traveled frequently, attended meetings and conventions, and was a regular visitor at the White House. She was a special guest at the inauguration of President Kennedy. Edith died in 1961 at the age of eighty-nine on Woodrow Wilson's birthday.

Florence Kling De Wolfe Harding

Served as First Lady during the term of her husband, Warren G. Harding, twenty-ninth President of the United States

BORN	August 15, 1860
PLACE OF BIRTH	Marion, Ohio
ANCESTRY	English, German
MOTHER	Louisa M. Bouton Kling (?-1893)
FATHER	Amos H. Kling (1832-1913)
HUSBANDS	Henry De Wolfe (1858-1894)
	Warren G. Harding (1865-1923)
CHILDREN	One boy
EDUCATION	Conservatory of Music, Cincinnati, Ohio
AGE AT INAUGURATION	61
YEARS AS FIRST LADY	1921-1923
DIED	November 21, 1924
CAUSE OF DEATH	Kidney disease

Florence Kling's father was the richest man in the small town of Marion, Ohio, where Florence was born. She grew into a fun-loving and independent young woman, gawky, plain and a bit reckless. She eloped with Henry De Wolfe in 1880, but the marriage didn't last long. Florence returned to Marion with her two-year-old son. Too proud to live with her parents again, she supported herself by giving piano lessons.

Florence married Warren Harding, editor of the local newspaper, in 1891. Her father was so upset that he boycotted the wedding and didn't speak to Florence for seven years. But Florence, who had her father's strong will and determination, did as she pleased. She had a head for business and took over the circulation department of her new husband's paper. Throughout their marriage, Florence stayed as close to her husband as possible. Yet, he managed to carry on two prolonged love affairs, one with Carrie Phillips and another with Nan Britton by whom he had a daughter.

Warren Harding's political career culminated in his election to the Presidency in 1921. Although he became one of the nation's most popular Presidents, opinions about the First Lady were mixed. Some members of Washington's society found Florence crude and domineering. Her brashness may have seemed inappropriate, but the White House with Florence as hostess was more accessible to the public than it had been in years. She even introduced herself to visitors touring the White House and personally escorted them.

Along with the usual White House parties and receptions, there were poker games upstairs, where Florence served liquor despite the Prohibition. She regularly visited war veterans in the hospital, and when she gave a Veterans' Garden Party on the White House lawn, she insisted on wearing her everyday hat so the veterans could easily recognize her.

The Hardings were both in poor health throughout their stay in the White House. They took an extended vacation to the west coast in the summer of 1923. The First Lady returned to the White House a widow, the President having died of a heart attack while they were in California. Florence returned to Marion to live quietly, but died just a year later.

Grace Anna Goodhue Coolidge

Served as First Lady during the term of her husband, Calvin Coolidge, thirtieth President of the United States

BORN	January 3, 1879
PLACE OF BIRTH	Burlington, Vermont
ANCESTRY	Unknown
MOTHER	Lemira Barrett Goodhue (1848-1929)
FATHER	Andrew Issachar Goodhue (?-1923)
HUSBAND	Calvin Coolidge (1872-1933)
CHILDREN	Two boys
EDUCATION	Burlington High School; University of Vermont
AGE AT INAUGURATION	44
YEARS AS FIRST LADY	1923-1929
DIED	July 8, 1957
CAUSE OF DEATH	Heart disease

Grace Goodhue and Calvin Coolidge were both born in Vermont. They met in Northampton, Massachusetts, where she taught at a school for the deaf and he was beginning his law career. They were an unlikely couple. He was quiet, severe, and rather glum; she was warm, friendly, and always cheerful. But they married in 1906 and had two sons. In the Coolidge household, Calvin was the provider and had little time for anything else. Grace cooked, cleaned, and cared for the children. Her husband felt she belonged at home and as his political career progressed did not allow her to attend his speeches. But Grace didn't mind being excluded from her husband's work and cheerfully fulfilled her role as wife and mother.

The Coolidges' simple lifestyle changed when he became Vice President in 1921. There were receptions, dinners, and parties to attend. There were politicians, celebrities, and diplomats to meet. Grace had no experience in the world of society but was so naturally charming that everyone liked her. She joked that her gift for sparkling discourse came from years of holding up both her end of the conversation and her husband's as well.

Calvin Coolidge became President upon Warren Harding's sudden death in 1923. Grace was apprehensive about being First Lady, but she took on her new job with diligence. She dressed in stylish outfits as fine clothes for his wife was the frugal President's one indulgence. Her schedule was packed with appointments, appearances, social affairs, and domestic details. Grace kept up with her White House duties even when her sixteen-year-old son died from blood poisoning.

Everyone in Washington loved Mrs. Coolidge. She was charming, cheerful, and kind to everyone. She stayed away from politics and made no attempt to influence her husband, and he never dreamed of discussing issues with her. With her natural social grace and her willingness to stay within the bounds of "traditional" feminine behavior, Grace Coolidge soon enjoyed comparisons to the beloved Dolley Madison.

Calvin Coolidge was elected to his own term as President, but chose not to run again four years later. Grace was happy to return to her private life in Northampton. After her husband's death in 1933, she remained active. She raised money for the school for the deaf, traveled to Europe, became an avid baseball fan, and spent much time with her son and her grandchildren. She died in 1957 at the age of seventy-eight.

Lou Henry Hoover

Served as First Lady during the term of her husband, Herbert C. Hoover, thirty-first President of the United States

BORN	March 29, 1874
PLACE OF BIRTH	Waterloo, Iowa
ANCESTRY	Irish, English
MOTHER	Florence Weed Henry
FATHER	Charles Delano Henry
HUSBAND	Herbert C. Hoover (1874-1964)
CHILDREN	Two boys
EDUCATION	San Jose Normal School (Class of 1894); B.A. from Leland Stanford University (1898), Stanford, California
AGE AT INAUGURATION	54
YEARS AS FIRST LADY	1929-1933
DIED	January 7, 1944
CAUSE OF DEATH	Heart Attack

Lou Henry grew up in the hills of southern California. She was an excellent horsewoman, and loved to hike and camp. Lou met Herbert Hoover in geology class at Stanford University. They found they had a lot in common. They both had been born in Iowa, they loved the outdoors, and they were both earning geology degrees. Herbert and Lou were married in 1899 and set off for China, where Herbert had a job with a mining company.

Hoover traveled all over the world as a geologist, with Lou always working by his side. They went from China to Burma, India, Egypt, and Australia, carrying their two babies in baskets. Lou loved this adventurous life and worked hard maintaining a household and helping her husband with his work. World War I found them in Western Europe, where they began working on various war relief projects.

When they finally returned home, the Hoovers were well known, politically experienced, and quite rich. Lou brought her formidable energies to Washington when Hoover was appointed to Harding's Cabinet in 1921. She became involved with several women's organizations, making speeches urging women to have their own careers and to get involved in politics. She even made brief speeches for her husband's Presidential campaign.

After Hoover became President in 1929, Lou filled the White House with objects from her travels and restored several neglected rooms. She insisted on the best of everything and gave elegant parties. The flow of guests was endless. There was often company for breakfast as well as lunch and dinner.

The Depression destroyed the First Family's lavish lifestyle and Hoover's bid for re-election as well. Although Lou was disappointed, she looked forward to returning to California. She was a lifelong supporter of the Girl Scouts. When the Hoovers left the White House, they gave their summer home in the Blue Ridge Mountains to the government for use by the Girl and Boy Scouts. In California she resumed her outdoor activities, occasionally spoke to women's groups, and got involved in community projects. She died from a sudden heart attack after attending a concert in New York, just before her seventieth birthday.

Anna Eleanor Roosevelt

Served as First Lady during the term of her husband, Franklin D. Roosevelt, thirty-second President of the United States

BORN	October 11, 1884
PLACE OF BIRTH	New York, New York
ANCESTRY	Dutch, English
MOTHER	Anna Hall Roosevelt (1863-1892)
FATHER	Elliott Roosevelt (1860-1894)
HUSBAND	Franklin Delano Roosevelt (1882-1945)
CHILDREN	Six: 5 boys, 1 girl
EDUCATION	Allenswood, Wimbledon, England
AGE AT INAUGURATION	48
YEARS AS FIRST LADY	1933-1945
DIED	November 7, 1962
CAUSE OF DEATH	Aplastic anemia

As a child, Eleanor Roosevelt felt homely and awkward. She adored her father, but he was banished from the family because of his drinking. By the time Eleanor was ten years old, both her parents had died and she and her brothers were sent to live with their strict maternal grandmother. Young Eleanor was a shy, unhappy child, full of insecurity and self-doubt.

At fifteen, Eleanor was sent to finishing school in England, and there she was nurtured and gained the confidence she needed. Upon her return home, she began working with poor people in the slums of New York City. On March 17, 1905, she married her distant cousin Franklin D. Roosevelt. Eleanor gave birth to six children in the next eleven years, one of whom died in infancy.

With her husband's election to the New York State Senate in 1910, Eleanor was introduced to politics. It wasn't until 1921, however, when her husband was stricken with polio, that her real political life began. Initially, Eleanor was tutored in politics in order to renew and stimulate her husband's waning political interests. But by 1928, when Franklin Roosevelt returned to the political arena as a candidate for governor of New York, Eleanor had become a public figure in her own right. She had been active in the League of Women Voters, the Women's Trade Union League, and the women's division of the Democratic party. She had learned to speak in public and to write political articles and had developed what would be a lifelong commitment to improve the lives of the oppressed and the underprivileged.

During Franklin Roosevelt's 2 terms as governor, Eleanor became her husband's "eyes and ears," visiting state institutions and reporting back to him. When Roosevelt became President of the United States in 1933, Eleanor expanded this role. She traveled extensively and lectured throughout the country. In addition, she had her own radio program and a syndicated daily newspaper column. She initiated weekly White House press conferences with women reporters. Becoming a major voice in her husband's administration, she worked for reforms to help racial minorities and the poor. Eleanor's liberal causes and activities made her both the most controversial and the most admired First Lady in history. More important, she developed the role of First Lady into a powerful and respected position.

After her husband's death, Eleanor's political life continued. She was appointed a member of the U.S. delegation to the United Nations by Presidents Truman and Kennedy. She was chairperson of the United Nations Human Rights Commission and a goodwill ambassador abroad. Eleanor Roosevelt was a tireless and influential advocate of human rights until her death in 1962.

Elizabeth Virginia Wallace Truman

Served as First Lady during the term of her husband, Harry S. Truman, thirty-third President of the United States

BORN	February 13, 1885
PLACE OF BIRTH	Independence, Missouri
ANCESTRY	English
MOTHER	Margaret Elizabeth Gates Wallace (1862-1952)
FATHER	David Willock Wallace (1860-1903)
HUSBAND	Harry S. Truman (1884-1972)
CHILDREN	One girl
EDUCATION	Barstow School for Girls, Kansas City, Missouri
AGE AT INAUGURATION	60
YEARS AS FIRST LADY	1945-1953
DIED	October 18, 1982
CAUSE OF DEATH	Heart failure

Born in Missouri in 1885, Bess Wallace loved to ride, skate, climb trees, and play baseball, and she was the best tennis player in town. She had many friends and at first barely noticed the attentions of bookish Harry Truman. When Bess and Harry became engaged in 1917, it had been seven years since he first proposed and it would be another two before their wedding. The bride and groom were both in their mid-thirties when they married. Bess had been active with her friends and helping her widowed mother take care of the household. Harry had tried various business ventures before finally going into politics. He became a Senator in 1934, and he, Bess, and their ten-year-old daughter went to Washington. Although Bess had never before left her hometown of Independence, Missouri, she liked Washington. She shared her husband's interests and helped him with his work. But Bess always hated the publicity that went with being a political wife.

When Harry Truman ran as Roosevelt's Vice President in 1945, Bess went to bed on election night before the results were settled. She resigned herself to being the wife of the Vice President, and dutifully attended the endless parties, luncheons, and dinners. Then Roosevelt died later that year, and Bess was suddenly the First Lady.

Bess preferred not to follow Eleanor Roosevelt's path. She didn't hold press conferences or champion any causes. She entertained only when necessary. Bess supervised White House menus, handled household expenses, and spent much of the day answering letters. While she still enjoyed a loving and intellectual partnership with her husband in private, publicly Bess preferred to stay in the President's shadow.

The Washington press was frustrated by Bess Truman for her favorite answer to reporters' questions was "No comment." The First Lady protected her privacy so well that she went Christmas shopping at Washington department stores alone and unrecognized.

At the end of her husband's second term, Bess could hardly wait to get out of the White House and back home. There she settled back into the privacy she preferred. She lived a quiet domestic life that remained unchanged even after Truman's death in 1972. Bess died in 1982 at the age of ninety-seven.

Always very close to her parents, the Trumans' daughter Margaret has written biographies of Harry and Bess Truman and has earned a reputation as an excellent murder mystery writer.

Mary Geneva Doud Eisenhower

Served as First Lady during the term of her husband, Dwight D. Eisenhower, thirty-fourth President of the United States

BORN	November 14, 1896
PLACE OF BIRTH	Boone, Iowa
ANCESTRY	Swedish and English
MOTHER	Elivera Carlson Doud (1878-?)
FATHER	John Sheldon Doud (1871-1951)
HUSBAND	Dwight David Eisenhower (1890-1969)
CHILDREN	Two boys
EDUCATION	East Denver High School; Miss Wolcott's Finishing School, Denver, Colorado
AGE AT INAUGURATION	56
YEARS AS FIRST LADY	1953-1962
DIED	November 1, 1979
CAUSE OF DEATH	Cardiac arrest

Mary Geneva Doud (called Mamie from birth) grew up in Denver, Colorado, with servants, elegant surroundings, and vacation trips. She met Dwight Eisenhower during a trip to Texas in 1915, and they were married a year later. Eisenhower was a young lieutenant beginning an army career. He and Mamie were married less than a month when he warned her that for him, she would always come second. His country came first.

Mamie made the best of her life. She didn't like the frequent moves as her husband went from post to post, and she never got used to his long absences. But she gave him the support he needed, managed their household efficiently, rarely complained, and didn't interfere with his work. She also had the social skills suited for an officer's wife. Mamie made her husband the center of her life, and Dwight could not have hoped for a better wife. They had two sons, but one died of scarlet fever when he was only three years old.

World War II made Dwight Eisenhower famous, but it made Mamie unhappy. She worked at the USO and wrote him often. She was proud of his position as Supreme Commander of the Allied Forces in Europe, but she feared for his safety. And he was away for three long years. Mamie was living in Washington, unhappy and often ill until the war ended and her husband came home.

Mamie was pleased and proud when her husband became President in 1953. She brought considerable household management skills to her job as First Lady. She added feminine touches to the White House decor. Although she had never had any experience in politics, Mamie was a popular First Lady because she represented what was then considered the ideal woman. She was innocent, cheerful, and wanted only to create a nice home and be a good wife and mother.

She managed the staff with the discipline of an army officer, but she remembered the birthday of each member of the White House staff, and they all received Christmas presents from the First Lady. Mamie considered it her job to make the White House a warm and comfortable place, and she never got involved in her husband's political sphere.

Having traveled much of their married life from the Panama Canal Zone to the Philippines and to Europe after World War II, Mamie spent much of her time during Ike's second term preparing their retirement home in Gettysburg, Pennsylvania. Here they retired in 1961. They lived together happily until Eisenhower's death eight years later. Mamie died in 1979.

Jacqueline Lee Bouvier Kennedy Onassis

Served as First Lady during the term of her husband, John F. Kennedy, thirty-fifth President of the United States

BORN	July 28, 1929
PLACE OF BIRTH	Southampton, New York
ANCESTRY	French, Irish
MOTHER	Janet Norton Lee Bouvier (1908-?)
FATHER	John Vernou Bouvier, III (1891-1957)
HUSBANDS	John Fitzgerald Kennedy (1917-1963)
	Aristotle Socrates Onassis (1906-1975)
CHILDREN	Three: 2 boys, 1 girl
EDUCATION	Vassar College; the Sorbonne; George Washington University, Washington, D.C. (1951)
AGE AT INAUGURATION	31
YEARS AS FIRST LADY	1961-1963

Jacqueline Bouvier spent part of her childhood in a large apartment in New York City and the rest of the time at an estate on Long Island. With her parents' divorce and her mother's remarriage, young Jackie enjoyed another elegant apartment in Washington and another summer estate in Rhode Island. Jackie attended Vassar, studied in Paris for a year, and then attended George Washington University. After graduating, she got a job writing a daily column for a Washington newspaper. One of her interviews was with Senator John F. Kennedy.

Jackie and John Kennedy had attended President Eisenhower's inauguration together. Later in 1953, 1,700 guests attended the Kennedys' gala wedding reception. Jackie wanted to be a good Senate wife and she helped her husband when she could, but Washington's political society held little interest for her. She preferred the company of artists and writers. When her husband ran for President, Jackie was surprised to discover that she enjoyed campaigning. Stylish and pretty, aristocratic and clever, mother of a toddler and pregnant again, Jackie was a big success with the voters.

The country fell in love with the young, attractive First Family that moved into the White House in 1961. Jackie stated that she intended to be a wife and mother, but she was soon announcing big changes for the White House. She wanted to restore the rooms with furnishings from the eras of past Presidents and make the White House a showcase of American art and history. Jackie enlisted the help of artists, museum curators, and historians. When her project was completed, she prepared a guide book and conducted a televised tour of the White House.

Jacqueline Kennedy intrigued the nation. She was as aloof and unapproachable as she was charming and chic, and she had the glamour of a Hollywood actress. The President was proud of his wife, but he wasn't always pleased with her interests. She usually refused to attend meetings and social events, insisting on her privacy, saying that her children needed her time and attention. Jackie was making a rare public appearance when she accompanied her husband to Dallas in 1963. She was at his side when he was assassinated, and, still wearing her blood-stained suit, witnessed the swearing-in of Lyndon Johnson. Jackie made the arrangements for John Kennedy's funeral. Millions of television viewers witnessed the solemn event and Jackie's strong, dignified presence.

Jackie remains among the best-loved women in the world long after leaving the White House. She still guards her privacy fiercely—a job that becomes increasingly difficult. She married Greek shipping tycoon Aristotle Onassis in 1969, and after he died, Jackie returned to New York City. She lives and works in New York as an editor for a major publishing company.

Claudia Alta Taylor Johnson

Served as First Lady during the term of her husband, Lyndon B. Johnson, thirty-sixth President of the United States

BORN	December 22, 1912
PLACE OF BIRTH	Karnack, Texas
ANCESTRY	English, Spanish, Scots
MOTHER	Minnie Lee Pattillo Taylor (1874-1960)
FATHER	Thomas Jefferson Taylor (1874-1960)
HUSBAND	Lyndon Baines Johnson (1908-1973)
CHILDREN	Two girls
EDUCATION	B.A., University of Texas (1933)
AGE AT INAUGURATION	50
YEARS AS FIRST LADY	1963-1969

When Claudia Taylor was a baby, her nurse said she was "pretty as a lady bird," and the nickname stuck. Although her mother died when she was five, Lady Bird had a happy childhood and grew into a quiet, modest young woman. At the University of Texas, where she studied art and journalism, she worked hard and was in the top ten of her graduating class.

Lyndon Johnson had already begun his political career when Lady Bird met him in 1934. He proposed to her the day after they met. Lady Bird hesitated, but not for long. They were married three months later. Since she had grown up with servants, she knew nothing about housekeeping, but she did her best to make a nice home for her husband. Lyndon Johnson was abrupt and demanding, but Lady Bird adjusted to his domineering ways. She decided that serving him breakfast in bed was easier than setting the table.

Lady Bird devoted herself to her husband's political career, and her quaint Southern charm won her many admirers. She was known for her even temper and calm manner, for her gracious hospitality and her kindness. She campaigned actively when Lyndon ran for the Senate, and helped him with his speeches as well. Lady Bird again campaigned extensively when her husband ran for Vice President. When President Kennedy was assassinated in 1963, she unexpectedly became First Lady.

There were barbecues and hootenannies as well as formal parties in the Johnson White House, but entertaining was not Lady Bird's first concern. She visited depressed areas of the country in her fight against poverty. She suggested women for government posts, attended meetings of women's organizations, and wrote articles about women in American society. Her biggest cause, however, was to clean up and beautify the country. She sponsored conferences, gave speeches, dedicated parks, and traveled widely in her efforts to make a more beautiful America.

Both of their daughters were married while the Johnsons lived in the White House. But the continuing war in Vietnam began to erode the public's support of the Johnsons. Lady Bird as well as the President became a target for anti-war protests. When Johnson chose not to run for a second term, Lady Bird was relieved. They retired to Texas, where Johnson died four years later. Lady Bird soon became as active as she had been as First Lady. She worked for all her favorite causes, founded the National Wildflower Research Center, and continues to support numerous environmental organizations. Lady Bird Johnson remains among the best loved and most accomplished of all the First Ladies.

Thelma Catherine Ryan Nixon

Served as First Lady during the term of her husband, Richard M. Nixon, thirty-seventh President of the United States

BORN	March 16, 1912
PLACE OF BIRTH	Ely, Nevada
ANCESTRY	Irish, German
MOTHER	Katharina Halberstadt Bender Ryan (?-1930)
FATHER	William Ryan (?-1930)
HUSBAND	Richard Milhaus Nixon (1913-)
CHILDREN	Two girls
EDUCATION	University of Southern California
AGE AT INAUGURATION	56
YEARS AS FIRST LADY	1969-1974

Thelma Ryan was born on the eve of St. Patrick's Day, so her father always called her Pat. She learned early in life to work hard and keep smiling, even when life was hard. She grew up on a small farm in California, where there were few luxuries and little time to play. But Pat found ways to make farm work tolerable. When she was thirteen, her mother died, and Pat took over the housekeeping in addition to her farm chores and school work. Her father died five years later. Pat was on her own now, and she put herself through college by holding a variety of odd jobs. She became a high school teacher in Whittier, California, in 1937.

Pat met Richard Nixon, a lawyer, when they both joined a local theater group. She didn't take his attentions seriously at first—she was having too much fun with her activities and her friends. But the young lawyer finally won his case, and Pat married Richard Nixon in 1940. He continued his law practice, and she kept teaching until World War II took her husband overseas. When he returned, Richard Nixon decided to run for Congress.

Pat didn't like politics and dreaded being a political wife. But she knew that her husband's ambition was to be President, so she resolved to help him however she could. She took care of their home and two daughters alone. Pat refused to make speeches or offer opinions on issues, but she tirelessly organized campaign literature, handed out leaflets, solicited contributions, and handled the mail. She felt her husband could do great things, and it was her job to take care of the endless tasks so he could concentrate on the important matters. Pat gritted her teeth, swallowed her objections, and worked hard during her husband's political campaigns. Richard Nixon became a Congressman, then a Senator. In 1952 he was elected Vice President, and seventeen years later he was inaugurated President.

Pat was surprised to find that she enjoyed being First Lady. She liked being a hostess and she entertained dignitaries and ordinary people alike. Pat was gracious and cheerful, although she never became accustomed to being a public figure. When Richard Nixon was Vice President, Pat had made many goodwill tours to foreign countries, and this remained her greatest pleasure as First Lady. Although she didn't write, make speeches, support causes or even take on a pet project, she publicly encouraged people—particularly women—to get involved in volunteer work.

The Watergate crisis swiftly ended any pleasure Mrs. Nixon found as First Lady. Her husband's long efforts to stabilize the American economy and end military action against North Vietnam were ignored. Daughters Julie, who had married President Eisenhower's grandson David, and Tricia, who had been married at the White House in 1971, lent their support. But when the President resigned, Pat Nixon was bitter and distraught. Not long after the Nixons retired to San Clemente, she suffered the first of several strokes. The Nixons now live in New Jersey, with their children and grandchildren nearby.

Elizabeth Bloomer Warren Ford

Served as First Lady during the term of her husband, Gerald R. Ford, thirty-eighth President of the United States

BORN	April 8, 1918
PLACE OF BIRTH	Chicago, Illinois
ANCESTRY	Unknown
MOTHER	Hortense Neahr Bloomer (?-1948)
FATHER	William Stephenson Bloomer (1894-1934)
HUSBANDS	William C. Warren (1909-?)
	Gerald R. Ford (1913-)
CHILDREN	Four: 3 boys, 1 girl
EDUCATION	Bennington College, Vermont
AGE AT INAUGURATION	56
YEARS AS FIRST LADY	1974-1977

Betty Bloomer planned to be a professional dancer. After a pleasant childhood in Grand Rapids, Michigan, she went to college in Vermont to study dance. Then she moved to New York City and began dancing with Martha Graham, working occasionally as a model to pay her living expenses. But she found that she didn't have the dedication it took to be a professional dancer in New York City. Back home in Grand Rapids, Betty taught modern dance, started her own dance company, and became a fashion coordinator for a department store. She married William Warren in 1942, but the marriage ended in divorce five years later. She had no children by her first husband.

Soon after her divorce, Betty met Gerald Ford. Although they both approached their relationship cautiously, they fell in love and were married in 1948. Gerald was in the midst of his Congressional campaign, and Betty quickly learned that being a politician's wife often meant being without a husband at her side. They lived in Washington, where Betty took care of the house and the children, helped out in her husband's congressional office, and endured Gerald Ford's long and frequent absences. Betty was happily anticipating her husband's retirement from politics when Vice President Agnew resigned and President Nixon named Gerald Ford as the new Vice President.

Betty enjoyed being Second Lady because she was able to spend more time with her husband. When Nixon's resignation eight months later made Gerald Ford President, Betty was prepared. She blossomed in the White House. She had always been outspoken and loved an audience; now, as First Lady, people were listening to her. Betty's frankness won her criticism and popularity and provided a favorite slogan in Ford's re-election campaign: "Betty's Husband for President."

She quickly changed the formal and somber White House into a friendly and cheerful place. But hostessing was not her first concern. She was dedicated to supporting the arts and to improving the lives of handicapped children and the elderly. She strongly supported the Equal Rights Amendment, and was the most outspoken advocate of women's rights who ever lived in the White House.

Betty publicly took a liberal stand on many social issues. Her controversial opinions and her frank way of expressing them often caused a storm of reaction, but in the end most of the response was favorable. People were further impressed when Betty openly discussed the mastectomy she underwent in 1974. The First Lady wanted to educate and reassure women about breast cancer.

Betty was unhappy when her husband lost his bid for election as President in his own right. Retirement in California took away the sense of purpose she'd felt as First Lady, and she became dependent on alcohol and the painkillers she took for arthritis. Betty bravely announced her addiction to the public, hoping to encourage people with similar problems to seek professional help. After completing her treatment, she helped found the Betty Ford Center for Drug and Alcohol Rehabilitation. Betty continues to work to help others overcome disability, disease, and addiction.

Eleanor Rosalynn Smith Carter

Served as First Lady during the term of her husband, James E. Carter, thirty-ninth President of the United States

BORN	August 18, 1927
PLACE OF BIRTH	Plains, Georgia
ANCESTRY	English
MOTHER	Allethea Murray Smith (1905-)
FATHER	Wilburn Edgar Smith (1896-1940)
HUSBAND	James E. Carter (1924-)
CHILDREN	Four: 3 boys, 1 girl
EDUCATION	Georgia Southwestern College, Americus, Georgia
AGE AT INAUGURATION	50
YEARS AS FIRST LADY	1977-1981

Rosalynn Smith and Jimmy Carter knew each other almost all their lives. They both grew up in Plains, Georgia, and shared common values of hard work, church, and family. Rosalynn was in college before she really noticed Jimmy, who was several years older than she. A courtship began when Jimmy came home on leave from the Navy, and he and Rosalynn were married the following year, in 1946.

As a nineteen-year-old Navy wife, Rosalynn loved her new life. She had never been far from home before and her husband was often away, but she learned to run her household with ease. Later, as their children were born, she was proud of how well she managed motherhood. When Jimmy Carter left his Navy career to return to Plains to take over his family's business, Rosalynn was apprehensive about going home and losing her independence. But soon she was managing the office of the Carter wholesale peanut enterprise and knew more about the business than anyone in the family.

When Jimmy Carter was elected Governor of Georgia, Rosalynn cultivated new skills. She entertained important people, worked to improve services for mentally retarded children, and became comfortable making speeches. By the time her husband ran for President, Rosalynn was touring the country by herself, making speeches on his behalf while he was campaigning elsewhere.

In the White House, President and Mrs. Carter considered themselves equal partners. In many ways, Rosalynn was similar to Eleanor Roosevelt. Rosalynn discussed policies with her husband and reported back to him with information she gathered in her travels. She attended meetings and often acted as her husband's ambassador. But unlike Eleanor Roosevelt, Rosalynn preferred to remain an extension of her husband and didn't cultivate a public life of her own.

But she did have her own agenda. Rosalynn encouraged her husband to appoint a Commission on Mental Health, of which she became honorary chairperson. She worked to improve services for the elderly also. She supported women's causes and gave the President lists of women qualified to fill government posts. Before long, Rosalynn put her energies back on the campaign trail and worked long and hard for her husband's re-election campaign. After his 1980 defeat, Rosalynn returned to Plains disappointed and determined to direct her energies to social causes.

It wasn't long before the Carters were enjoying their retirement. Each wrote an autobiography, followed by a book they wrote together. The Carters still live in Georgia, where they continue to be active in social programs.

Anne Frances Robbins Davis Reagan

Served as First Lady during the term of her husband, Ronald Reagan, fortieth President of the United States

BORN | July 6, 1921
PLACE OF BIRTH | New York, New York
ANCESTRY | English
MOTHER | Edith Luckett Robbins Davis (?-1987)
FATHER | Kenneth Robbins
STEPFATHER | Loyal Davis
HUSBAND | Ronald Wilson Reagan (1911-)
CHILDREN | Two: 1 boy, 1 girl
EDUCATION | Smith College (class of 1943), Northampton, Massachusetts
AGE AT INAUGURATION | 59
YEARS AS FIRST LADY | 1981-1989

Nancy's mother and stepfather gave her the best of everything. They took her to the best restaurants, introduced her to wealthy people, bought her fine clothes, and sent her to good schools. But it wasn't always like that for young Nancy. Her parents divorced when she was just two, and she lived for five years with an aunt and uncle while her mother worked as an actress. The name Nancy was her mother's nickname for her. When Nancy was seven, Mrs. Robbins married Loyal Davis, a neurosurgeon who eventually adopted Nancy, and the happy new family settled in Chicago.

Nancy majored in drama in college and began an acting career when she graduated. With her talent and her mother's contacts in show business, Nancy got parts on both stage and screen. In 1949 she was introduced to Ronald Reagan, President of the Screen Actors Guild, who had recently become separated from his wife. Ronald Reagan and Nancy were married two years later. Nancy had always said that her greatest ambition was to have a happy marriage, and she abandoned her acting career and concentrated on being a wife and mother.

Ronald Reagan continued his acting career, but was gradually shifting toward politics. He became Governor of California in 1967, and Nancy was glamorous and chic as the Governor's wife. Many Californians accepted Nancy's high style, but the same style was widely criticized when she became First Lady in 1981.

In her first year in the White House, Nancy redecorated the living quarters, bought expensive new china, and appeared in public in expensive jewelry and costly designer clothing. Elegance and expensive taste had always been Nancy's trademark, much as it had been Jacqueline Kennedy's. But while Nancy bought fine clothes and furnishings, the country was worried about recession and unemployment.

Nancy changed her image. It was announced that her designer clothes were on loan and would be given to museums. She took on a cause: fighting drug abuse among young people. In her campaign for "a drug-free America," Nancy traveled around the country visiting rehabilitation centers, making speeches, and attending conferences. She was also active in supporting the Foster Grandparents Program. Criticized for being overprotective of the President during his recovery from an assassination attempt and during his recovery from surgery to remove intestinal growths, Nancy gained respect and sympathy after her surgery for breast cancer.

Nancy became widely admired and was taken seriously enough for some to wonder if she had too much influence over the President. But Nancy's interest in politics extended only to her husband's welfare. She talked to him, supported him, and counseled him, but insisted that the President's decisions were his own. Nancy did her best to look after her husband, and to promote her concern for home and family throughout the country. After two Presidential terms, the Reagans retired to their California ranch.

Barbara Pierce Bush

Served as First Lady during the term of her husband, George Bush, forty-first President of the United States

BORN	June 8, 1925
PLACE OF BIRTH	Rye, New York,
ANCESTRY	English
MOTHER	Pauline Robinson Pierce (1896-1949)
FATHER	Marvin Pierce (1893-?)
HUSBAND	George Herbert Walker Bush (1924-)
CHILDREN	Six: 4 boys, 2 girls
EDUCATION	Ashley Hall Preparatory School, Charleston, South Carolina
AGE AT INAUGURATION	63
YEARS AS FIRST LADY	1989-1993

Barbara grew up comfortably in Rye, New York. She attended Smith College for two years, but left when she married George Bush in 1945. Because of George Bush's many jobs in business and government, Barbara, her husband, and their children lived in seventeen different cities in the years since their marriage. The seemingly perfect family had its share of sorrow, including the 1953 death of daughter Robin from leukemia.

The White House became Barbara's home in 1989. She was determined to lead a normal life there and to keep doing what she had always done: run the house, take care of her husband, and spend time with her children and grandchildren.

Barbara Bush was perceived as a down-to-earth woman. Her wardrobe was unpretentious, she wore little make-up, and she refused to color her gray hair. Accustomed to speaking her mind, Barbara said that as First Lady she tried to learn to curb her tongue. She preferred to leave politics to her husband. If she disagreed with him, she did so only in private; she felt that her job was to support the President in public. She was not interested in becoming involved with government policy-making. The First Lady was devoted to a special cause, however: national literacy.

Convinced that the nation's social, economic, and political problems were all linked to the high rate of illiteracy, Barbara worked with many organizations to promote literacy for all Americans. She wanted to increase public awareness of the problem and encourage people to volunteer in the fight against illiteracy. Barbara volunteered her services to various social causes over the years, and felt that as First Lady she had the opportunity to make a difference. With her natural charm and common sense attitude, she did.

Hillary Rodham Clinton

Serving as First Lady during the term of her husband, William J. Clinton, forty-second President of the United States

BORN	October 26, 1947
PLACE OF BIRTH	Chicago, Illinois
ANCESTRY	English, Welsh, French, Scottish
MOTHER	Dorothy Howell (1919-)
FATHER	Hugh Rodham (1911-)
HUSBAND	William J. Clinton (1946-)
CHILDREN	One girl
EDUCATION	Wellesley College (1969); J.D. (1973) Yale University
AGE AT INAUGURATION	45
YEARS AS FIRST LADY	1993-

Hillary Rodham spent her childhood in Park Ridge, Illinois, where her father ran a textile company. At Wellesley College she was president of the student government and gave a commencement address that gained her nation-wide media attention.

While studying for her law degree at Yale University, she first met Bill Clinton. When they married and moved to Arkansas in 1975, Hillary became a political partner as well as a wife. Bill Clinton was elected governor of Arkansas in 1978, the first of five terms he would serve in that office. Hillary taught at the Schools of Law at the University of Arkansas in Fayetteville and Little Rock, and joined the Rose Law Firm.

Her interest in public education and the rights of children soon made Hillary a prominent force in state congressional issues. She chaired the Arkansas Education Committee which recommended substantial reforms in accreditation standards for the state's public schools. As an author and lecturer, Hillary has spoken out on issues affecting families and the changing roles of women. As a working mother, she knows the challenge of caring for her daughter while continuing her own active career.

Hillary has served on many civic and corporate boards and has twice been named to the National Law Journal's list of the 100 most influential lawyers in America. As First Lady, Hillary wants to use her professional background and expertise to continue helping to resolve problems. She likes bringing people together around issues and talking through them until solutions are reached.

Joel Iskowitz

The White House

A History of the White House

Every president, with the exception of George Washington, has lived at 1600 Pennsylvania Avenue. Plans for the construction of what was then known as the President's House began during George Washington's administration—as did plans for the entire city of Washington, D.C. The President's House was to be both a suitable dwelling for the chief executive and his family and a place where foreign rulers and diplomats could be received in style.

The Commissioners of the Federal City (Washington) established two architectural competitions in 1791. By July 1792, a gold medal was awarded to James Hoban, a resident of Charleston, South Carolina, for his designs of the mansion. The exterior design reflected the Palladian architecture of mid-18th century Europe, but the house was to undergo many changes from Hoban's original plans.

Although the work progressed slowly, President John Adams and his family were able to move into the unfinished mansion in 1800. Mrs. Abigail Adams described the uncompleted President's House in a letter to her daughter:

> "The house is made habitable but there is not a single apartment finished. . . . We have not the least fence, yard or other convenience, without, and the great unfinished audience-room" (today the East Room) "I make a drying room of, to hang up the clothes in. The principal stairs are not up and will not be this winter."

Thomas Jefferson described the house as "Big enough for two emperors, one Pope and the grand lama." Architect Benjamin Henry Latrobe was hired by Jefferson to assist him in completing the unfinished building. Latrobe was responsible for changes in Hoban's original design. The influence of Jefferson's preferences appeared as pavilions and elegant terraces which concealed such functional necessities as hen houses, laundry rooms, and storerooms.

Inside the mansion, Jefferson decorated with ideas from the continent. Where the Adams' taste was decidedly English, Jefferson preferred French furnishings as well as French food. This trend toward elegance was continued by Dolley Madison, wife of President James Madison.

Many of the early furnishings at the President's House were lost when the British burned Washington during the War of 1812. The big house would have been totally destroyed by that fire in 1814 if it hadn't been for a providential rainstorm which put out the flames. In rebuilding the burned-out shell, white paint was used on the exterior to cover the traces of the fire. The name "White House" was not officially adopted until 1901, but it was known as the White House from 1816 on.

By 1816, President and Mrs. James Monroe moved into the mansion—now rebuilt but still largely unfurnished. New furniture was ordered, and eventually the White House was again an elegant place for the President and his family to live and receive the nation's guests.

During succeeding administrations, the country's presidents and their wives made changes to the executive mansion. Mary Todd Lincoln was publicly criticized for the amount of Federal money used to improve the White House during the Civil War. Frances Folsom Cleveland was married in the White House, and Caroline Lavinia Scott Harrison collected examples of the china used by previous administrations.

When Theodore Roosevelt became president, Edith Roosevelt and their six children took up residence with him in the White House. It was a time of pony rides, wrestling matches, and children's voices echoing in the high-ceilinged rooms. But it was also a time of change. Mrs. Roosevelt hired architects to handle a major remodeling of the building in 1902. This remodeling was a return to the simple, classical lines of the original building.

During World War I, grazing flocks of sheep were seen on the White House lawn—President Woodrow Wilson wanted to free manpower needed for the war effort.

By 1927, the roof of the White House was in need of repair. Under President Calvin Coolidge, the roof was raised high enough to add an extra floor to the mansion. This renovation actually weakened the structure, and President Truman ordered extensive remodeling and repairs which began in 1949 and were completed in 1952. These were the last major repairs done on the White House to date.

Inside the White House

In this brief history of the White House, it is not possible to describe the entire mansion. All of the presidents who have lived here left something of themselves in this, the most famous house in the United States. A visitor to Washington, D.C., who takes a tour of the White House will surely see some of the rooms listed below. The visitor is most fortunate to have walked the same halls as all but one of the Presidents of the United States and their families.

The East Room

One of the first rooms the visitor to the White House will see is the elegant East Room, decorated in white and gold with shining parquet floors. In this room, official receptions are held as well as some news conferences. Here, too, the seven presidents who died in office lay in state.

When the President holds formal dinners in the State Dining Room and plans entertainment afterward, this entertainment is frequently held in the East Room—a suitable setting for plays, concerts, and recitals. The Modern East Room is a far cry from the place Abigail Adams used many years ago to hang out her laundry.

The Green Room

Although it was originally planned as a dining room, today the Green Room is a parlor. Its walls are covered with moss-green watered-silk, and it looks much as it did in the early 19th century. The Green Room could be called a Federal parlor in a traditional classic style. Furnished with pieces from the Jeffersonian era, the Green Room was the favorite room of President John F. Kennedy.

The Blue Room

The walls of this formal reception room are hung in a cream-striped satin, but the color blue is in the hangings, the wainscoting, and the furniture. The view from the windows of this room shows the south grounds of the White House with the impressive Jefferson Memorial in the background. The color blue is accented with gold in both the draperies and the upholstery used on the furniture.

The Red Room

Still another parlor or sitting room, the walls of the Red Room are hung in cerise silk, and the furniture is upholstered in the same. Accents of gold are used here in much the same way as in the Blue Room. The Red Room is a good example of the American Empire period, circa early 1800s.

The State Dining Room

During a formal state dinner, this white and gold room can seat as many as 150 guests. A large, well-known portrait of Abraham Lincoln hangs over the fireplace, looking out at the assembled guests. When the table or tables are set for dinner, the array of fine linens, china, and silverware, as well as the many crystal glasses, make quite an impressive sight.

The Lincoln Bedroom

Abraham Lincoln used this room as his Cabinet Room. It was here that he signed the Emancipation Proclamation on January 1, 1863, freeing southern slaves. Today, this room includes the ornate mahogany bed once used in the state guest chamber. Much of the other furniture in this room came from the Lincoln era in the White House.

The Queen's Bedroom

During the 20th century, queens visiting the United States from Great Britain, the Netherlands, and Greece were accommodated in this room. Its decor of red, rose, and white offers a pleasant, regal setting.

The rooms described here are only some which have been used throughout the history of the White House. Each room includes many original pieces as well as excellent copies of period pieces. The china collection, the furniture, and the many great paintings throughout the mansion are all worthy of individual study in themselves. A visit to the nation's capital cannot be called complete unless it includes a visit to the President's home—The White House.